"As we look around all corners of the globe, feminism is in action. This accessible text introduces the reader to the most contemporary subjects and crucially asks critical organizational questions that benefit from the engagement with feminism."

— **Alison Pullen**, *Macquarie University, Australia*

"Business and feminism may seem an unlikely combination at first glance. This wonderfully innovative and readable book brings them together to great effect. Celia Harquail provides all of the tools needed to really make a feminist difference at work."

— **Scott Taylor**, *Birmingham University, UK*

FEMINISM

In this concise book, feminist thought is made accessible and relevant to both students and management practitioners. An empowering introduction to an often-overlooked key idea, this book illuminates how feminist thinking can liberate our understanding of work and management.

Feminism: A Key Idea for Business and Society boldly challenges assumptions about both feminism and business. It offers a primer on feminism for business and explains feminist interventions including adding women's voices, pushing for equality, and practicing feminist values to make businesses more successful and more just. It analyzes the obstacles organizations and individuals face in their efforts to address gender inequality, and demonstrates how feminist interventions have changed the terms of business conversations around topics such as defining work, centering the economy around care, how jobs work and wages are gendered, violence in the workplace, horizontal and peer-to-peer organizational structures that don't depend on dominance, enlightened leadership models, and power. As this book demonstrates, feminism has already had a profound impact on business, with many of its key tenets incorporated into business thinking.

As one of the first books to offer feminist insights and critiques of business to the practicing manager, business student, and non-academic, this book offers a fresh, positive vision that is remarkably relevant.

Celia V. Harquail, PhD, is co-founder of Feminists at Work and co-producer of Entrepreneurial Feminist Forums. She consults and writes about feminist business practice, and has taught at the Darden Graduate School of Business, UVA and Stevens Institute of Technology.

Key Ideas in Business and Management

EDITED BY STEWART CLEGG

Understanding how business affects and is affected by the wider world is a challenge made more difficult by the disaggregation between various disciplines, from operations research to corporate governance. This series features concise books that break out from disciplinary silos to facilitate understanding by analysing key ideas that shape and influence business, organizations and management.

Each book focuses on a key idea, locating it in relation to other fields, facilitating deeper understanding of its applications and meanings, and providing critical discussion of the contribution of relevant authors and thinkers. The books provide students and scholars with thought-provoking insights that aid the study and research of business and management.

Hierarchy
A Key Idea for Business and Society
JOHN CHILD

Feminism
A Key Idea for Business and Society
CELIA V. HARQUAIL

For more information about this series, please visit: www.routledge.com/Key-Ideas-in-Business-and-Management/book-series/KEYBUS

FEMINISM

A KEY IDEA FOR BUSINESS AND SOCIETY

Celia V. Harquail

Routledge
Taylor & Francis Group

LONDON AND NEW YORK

First published 2020
by Routledge
2 Park Square, Milton Park, Abingdon, Oxon OX14 4RN

and by Routledge
52 Vanderbilt Avenue, New York, NY 10017

Routledge is an imprint of the Taylor & Francis Group, an informa business

British Library Cataloguing-in-Publication Data
A catalogue record for this book is available from the British Library

Library of Congress Cataloging-in-Publication Data
Names: Harquail, Celia V., author.
Title: Feminism: a key idea for business and society / Celia V. Harquail.
Description: Abingdon, Oxon; New York, NY: Routledge, 2019. | Series: Key ideas in business and management | Includes bibliographical references and index.
Identifiers: LCCN 2019009030 | ISBN 9781138315099 (hardback) | ISBN 9781138315181 (pbk.) | ISBN 9780429456503 (ebook)
Subjects: LCSH: Sex discrimination in employment. | Sex role in the work environment. | Feminism. | Equality.
Classification: LCC HD6060 .H369 2019 | DDC 331.4–dc23
LC record available at https://lccn.loc.gov/2019009030

ISBN: 978-1-138-31509-9 (hbk)
ISBN: 978-1-138-31518-1 (pbk)
ISBN: 978-0-429-45650-3 (ebk)

Typeset in Joanna
by Deanta Global Publishing Services, Chennai, India

CONTENTS

ACKNOWLEDGMENTS

Loving thanks to my spouse Todd and my daughter Evangeline for their social reproductive work caring for me while I wrote, and to my daughter India for her intrepid research assistance. Deep gratitude to Petra Kassun-Mutch, Golnaz Golnaraghi, and especially my co-founder Lex Schroeder of Feminists at Work, for inspiring me as they put feminist leadership into practice. Heartfelt affection and appreciation for Liz O'Donnell, Cali Yost, Lili Powell, Ellen Poteet, Julia Harquail, Barbara Orser, Jody Suden, Susan Helman, Jennifer Brown, Ian Ayres, and Lizette Clarke for believing in the importance of this work and demonstrating this by supporting me. I am indebted to Terry Clague's prescient idea-spotting. I acknowledge that I work and live in the traditional homelands of the Ojibwe, Potawatomi, and Odawa peoples. This project is in partnership with my sisters and siblings in the community of entrepreneurial feminists that stretches from Vancouver to Manhattan and across the internet, all of whom are building businesses that provide life-affirming products to customers, just returns to investors, and right livelihoods to employees and owners, while advancing all of us towards flourishing.

INTRODUCTION TO FEMINIST INTERVENTIONS IN MANAGEMENT AND BUSINESS

Unequal. Tense. Unrequited. Antagonistic. Awkward. These are polite attempts to describe the relationship between business and feminism. These two perspectives on the world don't seem to have much between them that might support a positive connection. They have no common background, no mutual admiration, and no shared enemy to bring them together. As you may have wondered yourself, it's not even clear that the two perspectives should have a relationship at all.

Their relationship, if we can call it that, has always been lopsided. For decades and decades, feminism has been calling for business to transform how it operates. Feminism has asked business to include the perspectives of women in its considerations, to provide women and all people equal opportunities for paid employment and decision-making authority, and to transform what business prioritizes and defines as success. Business has attempted to quiet feminism by responding begrudgingly and only selectively. While feminism has struggled to get business's attention, business has dismissed feminism's presence as largely irrelevant, and waved away feminism's fundamental critiques.

The awkward relationship between business and feminism – this discomfort and lack of mutual engagement – seems predictable given how disparate their concerns appear to be. Business cares about making things efficiently and selling things profitably to create wealth for businesses' owners. Feminism cares about ending oppression and establishing equality to create a world in which all people flourish. These two perspectives don't speak the same language.

Their unequal efforts to connect make sense when we compare their cultural power. Business is more influential, hegemonic even, with an authority and importance that nearly everyone takes for granted and that business does not want challenged. Feminism is the tenacious upstart always contesting the status quo with impertinent questions, trifling concerns, and unrealistic expectations.

Their relationship goals are different too. Feminism is clear that it needs to engage with business to enroll business as an ally in transforming the world. Feminism needs to infiltrate business, divert business from its focus on profits for a few, and encourage business to expand its intentions and contributions. Business, for its part, seems convinced that feminism is largely extraneous to its success. Business doesn't seem to need or think it needs anything from feminism. Business would prefer not to engage with feminism. So instead of building a relationship that helps them both grow, the connection between business and feminism is unequal and unsteady. Neither business nor feminism is able to draw on the relationship to fulfill its own or its partner's full potential.

As a person who has studied and practiced both business and feminism, I've long been perplexed by the awkwardness of their relationship. It's been obvious, to me at least, that business and feminism need each other. Feminism needs business to spread feminism's vision of inclusion, equality, and flourishing into the arena of daily work life, as well as into the organization of our larger economy. And business, of course, needs feminism for all the ways it could breathe new life into how we work, why we work, and what we create together. These two perspectives should be interacting with each other, sharing ideas, pooling resources, and collaborating to make the world a better place. But they aren't.

WHY DON'T BUSINESS PEOPLE SEEM INTERESTED IN FEMINISM?

Trying to diagnose this problematic (non)relationship, I've imagined business deliberately ignoring feminism, flexing its cultural muscle to elbow feminism off to the side. I've noticed how business treats feminism as a distraction and fails to take its proponents seriously. I've seen business act paternalistically, trying to placate women and advocates of feminism with empty assurances and minimal adjustment. I've begun to understand that many business people are wary of feminism because they see it as a threat to their power, their privilege, and their positions within the status quo. All of these dynamics are plausible reasons for business to distance itself from a relationship with feminism.

After years of teaching business students and coaching managers, I've come to realize that there's a simpler, more fundamental explanation for why business distances itself from feminism, an explanation that precedes these others:

> Most business people just don't know enough about what feminism really is to recognize that feminism might be valuable to business.

That business people don't know what feminism is may not be a failing of business people themselves. It's hard to find discussions of feminism that go beyond the entry level conceptualization that "feminism means equality for women." It's also hard to find literature about feminist perspectives that is written for business people. Although there is a growing body of research by feminist organizational and management scholars analyzing business, leadership, managerial, company, and industry issues, this academic work is not accessible to practicing managers and rarely recommends the kind of action steps that managers look for. More practitioner-oriented books that are purportedly about feminism and business (like Sandberg's *Lean In* [2013]) rarely offer new ideas worth sharing, much less real feminist insights. Rather, they come off as Davos-polished, TED-approved, more-of-the-same advice urging women to work (even) harder. And, alas, not enough business people set out to investigate current feminist ideas, such as Roxane Gay's *Bad Feminist* (2014) or Chimamanda Adichie's (2015) *We Should All Be Feminists*, much less crack the spines of classics like bell hooks' *Feminism is for Everyone* (2000) so that they might apply fundamental feminist analyses to their own local business situations.

Judging from the number of books sold about productivity, leadership, innovation, and economic trends, business people are quite interested in learning about topics they recognize as relevant to improving their companies. So it's a shame that more business people don't recognize how feminism might contribute to business's success. Feminism is a more incisive tool for diagnosing problems and a more provocative catalyst for envisioning a positive future than almost any other idea touted by the conventional management press. If business engages with feminism, together they can create tremendous value, far beyond what we'd get from a four-hour work week or another disrupted industry. And yet, business people – with the exception of you, readers – seem either uninterested in, or resistant to learning about, feminism.

I would be remiss if I failed to mention another obstacle blocking business from seeing opportunity in a relationship with feminism. Feminism has active, deep-pocketed, and structurally entrenched opponents. These stewards of the status quo, including conservative and antifemale political leaders and parties, lobbyists for monied interest groups, consultancies, and even the gatekeepers of "business conversation," willfully distort feminism's messages so they can bolster resistance to feminism, sustain the perception of feminism's irrelevance, and/or neuter feminism's efforts to influence business. Consider, for example, how the current feminist #MeToo movement has raised public awareness of real, widespread, and dangerous harassment of women by men at work, only to have the business press highlight how male managers now fear that meeting alone with women colleagues might damage their careers. Men's careers, that is.

Want a more systemic, longer-term example of distortion? Consider how these stewards handled feminism's earliest argument for the inclusion of women in business. When feminism initially pressed business to admit women into wage-earning and management positions, feminism argued that bringing women into business was a moral issue. Feminism asserted that women had a human right to experience the world and earn a living as full participants, decision-makers, and creators of value equal to men. But instead of stepping up to address the moral implications of treating men and women equally, stewards of the status quo twisted and shrank the moral argument for equality into a less transformational "business case" for women.

No longer acknowledged by business as a moral issue, women's unequal status is now described as a financial problem, a human resource constraint, or a threat to a company's competitiveness. The reason for bringing women into business has been disconnected from the idea of women as human beings of equal value to men and with equal claims on opportunities that business might provide. Lost because of this disconnection was not only the moral argument itself, but also our conviction that the moral argument for women and men's equality is even valid to make in a business context. Instead of a moral case for equality that supports a vision of full human agency for everyone, business now argues that including women matters not because women are human, but because women will help increase productivity, share price, and profits.

PROTECTING BUSINESS'S MAGIC CIRCLE

The stewards of the status quo recognize, even without understanding feminism, that promoting economic, social, and political justice for women and all people threatens the foundations of their privilege and power, in business and everywhere. They resist feminism and deflect feminist advocacy because they want to protect business's "magic circle."

The magic circle, a concept from game design, is the imaginary space where a game is played. In the magic circle, the game's unique rules displace reality by creating an artificial "reality." While in the real world we move according to the natural laws of physics, inside the magic circle of a game, our movements are controlled by the tilt of the joystick. Our view of the world is replaced by imagery on the screen. When we play a game, we accept the artificial "reality" of the magic circle and don't question the rules. We follow them.

Business has created its own magic circle, a version of reality that serves business itself. It has designed the rules by which we all play together to create products and earn our livings. We might prefer a different "reality" and we might prefer different rules, but when we're in "business," we're expected to follow the rules as given and without question.

Lest you think that the magic circle is simply a metaphor, consider how business has created rules about industrial waste and pollution. You've heard accountants and economists describe these as "externalities," a category of costs that are incurred by a business's actions that a business itself does not pay for. Instead, everyone else pays for the cleanup of toxic waste that business created. Why? Because accountants, economists, business people, and business itself all agree to accounting rules that designate these costs as externalities and put them off the balance sheet, outside the magic circle. Most people think this is perfectly normal, if they stop to think about it at all.

Business asserts that its rules prioritize only rationality, efficiency, and getting good work done, and not the interests of some over others. Business also imagines that its structures, processes, norms, and participants operate cleanly, free of the racism, sexism, classism, or other systems that take advantage of some groups of people to privilege others. Business is wrong on both counts. Its rules aren't efficient and rational. They are rigged to serve the interests of owners and top managers rather than to serve all of us fairly. Also, business doesn't operate apart from the systems of domination and privilege that structure our larger society. Biases are woven into business's magic circle, distorting how we understand and organize our jobs, our companies, and our industries. These biases even distort how we think about business itself.

Business has a powerful hold on our culture's definition of reality, and the stewards of the status quo aim to keep things that way. Business is heavily invested in maintaining the dominance of its worldview, not just in business, but also in the rest of life. It protects its own narrow interests by limiting what can be discussed and what's even considered possible, by controlling its magic circle.

FEMINISM IN THREE INTERVENTIONS

Outside business's magic circle, feminism labors to interrupt business as usual, to catch business's attention, and to engage business in conversation, in three ways:

1. *Feminism intervenes to bring the voices, experiences, and wisdom of women* workers, leaders, managers, and scholars into all conversations about business, so that all people's perspectives are valued.
2. *Feminism intervenes to advocate for gender equality,* as well as racial, class, and all social equality, so that business practice will reflect and advance justice.
3. *Feminism intervenes to promote feminist values* of equality, agency, whole humanness, generativity, and interindependence as guidelines for business priorities and actions so that business itself can thrive by supporting feminism's goal of a world where everyone flourishes.

Feminism's interventions aim to interrupt the status quo and then invite business to embrace a larger set of interests, values, and visions. Really, what's not to like about including all people, treating everyone as equally valuable, and having everyone thrive?

What's not to like, what is hard for business to bear, is how deeply feminism seeks to challenge and transform business's world view. Feminism digs down to rattle business's foundations, by questioning business's practices, priorities, and defining values. Challenging the narrowness and self-serving nature of business's core values, feminism promotes alternative goals and criteria for success (see Chapter 3, "Feminist interventions in core business concepts," for details). Feminism suggests ways to redesign how we organize together to make things, sell things, and provide for each other. Feminism encourages us to reshape the space that business inhabits in our culture, so that the magic circle that once was "business" can embrace the experiences and interests of women and all people and support collective flourishing. Feminism invites us to draw on all people's perspectives as well as on feminist values to reimagine what business could be, how business could define success more broadly, and how business could increase not only productivity and profit, but also human flourishing.

Business should carefully consider feminism's invitation, because the rules that business has constructed aren't working well anymore, if they ever did. Business's magic circle is broken.

Business is currently designed so that it serves the few and the powerful: owners and elite management. It creates and reinforces a hierarchy of participants where the largest group – employees, workers – is also the group with the fewest resources, the least power, the lowest share of the returns of productivity. Business practices are extractive rather than regenerative. They take value from the many to give more to the few, shift the burdens of risk from companies to individuals, decrease the quality of community life, and damage the planet.

Business expends much time and energy trying to fix problems like low employee engagement, anemic innovation, frivolous products, and work–family conflict that are caused by business's distorted rules. Band aid programs for high commitment workplaces, design thinking, and key performance indicators never get close to the root causes of business's flaws. Even the thought leaders who propose visions of a better workplace fail to address the entrenched power imbalances that keep most employees subordinated to the interests of the elite few, from which all these other problems stem. There's a lot of energy for tinkering at the margins to make things somewhat better, but little attention is paid to the ways that the whole system is defective.

Business as it is currently designed will never be able to embrace human equality. There is no solution to gendered inequalities in business that allow the rules in the magic circle to stay the same. No mentoring program, no leadership training, no fixing of the pipeline, no leaning in, no unconscious bias training – none of it will change businesses enough that women, men, and all members of a business are equal, paid well for their contributions, working on jobs with meaning and dignity, able to support families and community life, and treated with respect at work. Business simply isn't able to permit all people to have voice, agency, and authority. The current rules of business's magic circle make both democracy and equality impossible. In fact, there is no "business case" for human equality or human flourishing, because the goals of business are not the goals of a just society.

Business needs feminism, not simply to fix business's problems but to help business transform itself into a system for making things and providing for each other that respects and supports all people as equally valuable human beings.

As this book will help you see, changing business so that women and all people are respected as equally human means changing the ways we think about every element of managing a business. Feminism challenges how we think about who people are, what they care about, what they have to offer, how best to get them to contribute, and how best to lead them in the shared work of creating value. Feminism also challenges how we think about value itself, what contributes to value, how contributions to value should be compensated, and how humans' efforts (energy, meaning, life, time) to create value should be balanced against the importance of money and power. Feminism offers practices and visions that will help to heal the problems caused by business as it is currently understood. Feminism has a plan to transform the magic circle, to embrace the interests of every living creature and to promote a vision of flourishing for the whole. Feminism is out to change the rules of the game.

OVERVIEW OF THIS BOOK

The three chapters of this book map on to the three interventions of feminism:

1. Bringing in the voices of women and marginalized people;
2. Advocating for gender equality; and
3. Promoting feminist values and goals.

Chapter 1, "A primer on feminism for business: Defining feminism," brings in the voices of women and marginalized people by offering an introduction to feminism. This primer addresses the most significant challenge to applying feminism to business, which is that too few people have a full, accurate understanding of what feminism proposes. The primer offers a full definition of feminism, introduces feminist values and goals relevant to business, and explains how feminism unbundles patriarchy and sexism to reveal the patterns of gendering that manufacture a rationale for men to dominate women. It includes discussions about how equality should be understood, how feminists define truth and objectivity, and how feminism understands oppression and inequality. Thus equipped with a fuller understanding of what contemporary feminism advocates, we can consider how feminism invites us to understand business differently.

Chapter 2, "Obstacles and approaches to gender equality in business," considers the difficulties that businesses and individuals face in their efforts to move towards gender equality. What have organizations and working women themselves done to make businesses more gender equitable? Why haven't these approaches worked very well? The chapter first considers three conditions of this current cultural moment that hobble efforts to move towards gender equality at work. Neoliberalism and postfeminism raise questions about how feminism is relevant to business and if it is relevant at all. Organizations themselves have sexism encoded into their processes, cultures, and structures. Because business people don't understand how gender oppression is built into organizations, their organizational change efforts make only marginal progress. The chapter then evaluates the organizational and individual approaches taken to advance gender equality, and explains how their underestimation of the work to be done makes them ineffective change efforts.

Chapter 3, *"Feminist interventions in core business concepts,"* takes up the third feminist intervention by bringing feminist values and goals into conversations about core business topics. It begins by contrasting ways that feminism and conventional business understand the goals of business, how organizational coordination should be achieved, and what values should define success. Then it offers eight short essays on key conversations in business to demonstrate how raising feminist concerns and values has changed the terms of these conversations. As a group, these essays demonstrate a pattern of analysis that you can take forward to conversations about other business topics that aren't covered here.

TIPS TO HELP YOU MANAGE THE CONTRADICTIONS OF THIS BOOK

This book will seem to contradict many of the ideas it aims to represent. It is authoritative about a world-view that challenges authority, it rejects unearned privilege but is written by a privileged person, it simplifies an insanely complex set of ideas, it discusses only the North American/Western elements of a global movement, and it covers much too little of profoundly important conversations in management and business. Now that you are warned about these contradictions, consider how you want to experience them. These thoughts, below, might help:

1. *When it comes to defining feminism, we advocates of feminism have agreed to "let 1,000 flowers bloom."*
Feminists want people to own their understanding of feminism – to experience it, feel emotionally connected to it, take responsibility for it – and so we don't want to impose definitions that might inhibit people from coming to their own understanding. Use your own experience and authority to draw your own conclusions.

Moreover, as feminism's advocates see it, anyone's understanding of ideas and thus any proposed definition of feminism is always partial, never "complete," and never "objective." Any person's understanding of feminism will necessarily reflect their social context (e.g., academia, fashion, or agriculture), their social position (e.g., whether they have privilege, status, celebrity, or not), and their personal experience (what they've encountered, what they have reflected on, how they have reached out to consider other experiences, etc.). Feminism is a multi-vocal, plural, ongoing conversation. We want to hear each other's perspectives without needing to assert our own as the definitive version.

2. Feminism questions authority, and the imperious manner that authority often relies on.
Feminism's advocates are all too familiar with the dynamic where one group tells another group how to behave, what to think, and how the world should be, and forbids them to question any of it. Feminists resist the idea that any person or group can assert themselves as the definitive authority on a history that is not their own. Instead, feminists give priority and authority to each individual person and group in defining their experiences of the world. Of course, this doesn't mean that anything goes. There are important things one can't advocate as being feminist. For example, a woman who argues that men should have dominion over women isn't advocating feminism.

For these reasons, it goes against the grain for any individual advocate of feminism to suggest they are offering "the" definition of feminism or "the" primer on feminist thinking. However, some definitions of feminism are more specific, more general, more comprehensive, more systematic, more contemporary, more intersectional, etc. than others. Pay attention to the boundaries that feminist advocates themselves place on their ideas.

3. Treat these ideas as catalysts, not definitive explanations.
This sounds like wordplay, but hear me out. I'm not proposing the definitive definition of feminism. I'm offering a catalytic definition that's explicitly intended to trigger new thinking, by bringing in some elements you haven't thought of before and by remaining open to new ideas. These ideas may even provoke your critique. All of this is good.

This catalytic definition is not offered so that readers can compare this definition to one or two or three different definitions, and then dismiss feminism because there's no clear path to agreement. We're not trying to be tidy, we're not trying to be perfect – we're trying to learn how to change the world.

4. Work with others, because feminism is a collective project that requires learning with others, on behalf of the group and not just our individual selves.
Feminist advocates believe that we are accountable for learning from each other's experiences. We recognize that feminism asks us to challenge our own deep assumptions as well as our own privilege. We don't expect learning about feminism to be easy, and we expect this learning to change how we see ourselves in the world.

5. Be comfortable with superficial contradictions.
Writing about feminism is like being one of the hands in M.C. Escher's famous work *Drawing Hands*. In *Drawing Hands*, two hands are shown, each hand emerging from the pencil held in the other hand. Writing about feminism is like erasing with the leaded end of the pencil, since we are redefining the very words we use

to construct our arguments. We are critical of what the words conventionally represent, but use them while noting their limitations.

Examples of words that we use even as we re-inscribe what they mean include "man" and "woman." Even while I critique the concepts of man = male and woman = female, I still need to use these words to connote the social groups that they are generally understood to refer to. Understand that there are more categories than male or female, and more genders than man or woman. Social groupings of gender, race, ethnicity, sexual orientation, religion, and more all matter, even when I don't list all of them out.

6. Recognize the complex definitions of common terms.
Many times I'll define and qualify a term and from then on present the term unmodified. Once I explain a concept, take that richer understanding all the way through. For example:

- Whenever I use the term feminism, understand that I'm referring to intersectional feminisms, plural, that include addressing race, gender, sex, orientation, class, nationality, and other groupings. If I'm referring to White feminism, Black feminism, or liberal feminism, I'll state that specifically.
- Whenever I use the term women, understand that I'm including anyone who claims membership in this group, regardless of their race, class, sex, or other category memberships.
- Once "unearned privilege" is defined, all later mentions of privilege refer to that unearned, standard type. Where I want to refer to "legitimately earned privilege," I'll do that explicitly since this kind of privilege is less common.

7. Get comfortable using these words:
    Oppression. Liberation. Consciousness. Agency. Patriarchy. Equality. Equity. Privilege. Class. Racism. Justice.
To talk about changing our perspectives on management and business, we have to bring new terminology into business's magic circle. Words like "oppression" have been kept outside the management conversation because, even though oppression structures how people in the workplace interact, business's magic circle denies that oppression is relevant. By not using these words, management conversations and those who participate in them allow gendered bias and other forms of injustice free rein. Bringing words like these into the management conversation automatically challenges the way that the magic circle for business has been drawn, and for whose benefit.

8. Consider my social location and expertise as you contend with the ideas shared here.
My perspectives on feminism and management are inescapably embedded in my own personal experiences, in my social position, my nationality, and in my

unearned status. As a person in this world, I benefit from White privilege, from Western and American privilege, from heterosexual and cisgender privilege, and from middle-class economic privilege. These privileges have come to me without me having to work for them, and they influence my experience of the world and how I understand the world. They usually work without my consent and sometimes outside of my awareness.

I work from status and expertise that I've earned, through years as a management scholar, a feminist researcher, and a business school professor, not to mention as a consultant, an entrepreneur, an activist, and a feminist person in this world. This status and expertise I'll happily claim, because it informs my work and what I can offer you readers. I've been on my learning journey with feminism for a very long time, and I'm still and forever will be actively engaged in reading, writing, talking, listening, and learning more about how gender, race, class, and other social groupings that are used to subordinate some so that others can raise themselves into more power. I don't know everything, and I do know a lot of things, and these I will share with you.

My unearned privilege, my earned expertise, and my role as an author put me in a position where I have significant discretion over which feminist concepts to address, which writers and research to cite, and which topics to exclude from this particular book. I've tried to make my choices explicit, rather than reflections of unconscious bias.

To embrace feminist principles as I write means to embrace and amplify my own voice, my own authority, my own point of view, and my own experience – and to acknowledge this. I want to be careful not to perpetuate "logics of domination" by insisting that my voice (the voice given authority in this volume) be treated as the objective expression of "truth." To be clear, I'm not presenting myself as a "typical" feminist. No one elected me to speak on behalf of feminists as a group. See me instead as an advocate for feminist perspectives who is genuinely invested in improving business practice.

One of the opportunities offered by this particular Routledge series is the invitation to step away from presenting myself as an objective observer or an all-knowing expert. Instead, the invitation was to share a learned and strong point of view. Thus, I haven't tried to hide my conclusions, to dust tough concepts with sugar, or to mollycoddle you readers. You have my point of view to work with, to contend with, and to extend. Take my opinions, my lapses, my oversights, and my mistakes as invitations to dig deeper, and move forward on your own.

9. When you find you don't agree with me, take responsibility for pursuing your concerns.
If you find yourself noting that a perspective doesn't match what you've experienced or read before, that's part of the point of the book. It would be easy for you to critique any of the ideas I share on the basis of them being articulated by this

particular White, Western feminist. You could also criticize them (and me) for their limitations, for not including everything, for presuming to offer a generalized viewpoint, an expert viewpoint, a practitioner's viewpoint, an academic's priorities, and so on. It's possible to engage in an endless string of criticisms that this is "not enough" and "biased." That's a great way to keep yourself busy seeming to engage with the ideas here, but instead ignoring them. Don't do that.

Be comfortable with partiality. Be comfortable with simplification as a strategy to aid comprehension. Be comfortable with acknowledging bias and point of view without demanding a kind of objectivity that is, quite frankly, unachievable and a figment of Western thought leaders' imaginations.

These limitations don't make ideas weak; they make ideas real.

TWO CAVEATS

All of this said, I'll offer these ideas with two important caveats:

- Understand that you have to do your own work to engage with feminist ideas, try them out for yourself, connect them to other related ideas, and adopt them (or not) as they make sense to you. Consider that just because they don't apply to you or your experience doesn't mean they aren't valid, valuable, and truthful to someone.
- Understand the primer, the definition, and the critique to follow are catalysts for conversation and further learning, and absolutely not the last word on the subject of what feminism is and should be.

Finally, recognize that this book is intended to help you take a few steps towards contemporary feminist views of management and organizations. It would take more than one short book to build a solid, comfortable bridge connecting you with academic feminism and feminist management studies. Feminist management scholarship tends to be quite sophisticated, drawing on perspectives like postmodernism and materialism that are several steps removed both from mainstream management perspectives and from how most people have been taught to think. This book will point you towards this work, but will take a more practical, less scholarly approach to connecting feminism and management.

This book is intended for readers who are genuinely curious about feminism's application to management and business. It is decidedly not for readers who need to be cajoled into considering perspectives that challenge their comfort and privilege. This book is not for readers who question whether equality, justice, and flourishing are the priorities of human community. Rather, this book is for readers who are open to learning about feminist ideas and who are ready to consider feminist challenges to business's status quo. This book is for readers who want to consider new and better questions about what business could be, and who can imagine a world where effective businesses embody equality and justice.

As a business scholar, as a family member, and as a citizen, feminism offers too much for me not to advocate for it. I want the world to grow into a more just, a more joyful, and a more regenerative place. I believe that business offers us a potent context for meaningful change and a powerful mechanism for influence. I also believe that feminism, rightly understood, offers us a practical, comprehensive, and inspiring place to anchor our visions of a future where everyone and everything flourishes. Personally, I am heavily invested in helping feminism transform how we think about working together to make things, earn our livelihoods, and support our lives. I hope that you'll feel inspired by the ideas advanced in this book, and put them to work yourself.

1

A PRIMER ON FEMINISM FOR BUSINESS

INTRODUCTION

Feminism is a complex, comprehensive perspective on how the world ought to be that makes room for many points of view. And yet, to write about feminist critiques of business and envision a feminist future, we need a simple, direct definition of feminism and a set of core principles that feminists use to guide how we should work together in relationships, in society, and especially in organizations. This first chapter offers a working definition of feminism to serve as a catalyst for conversation, distinguishes between protective and constructive feminism, establishes the parameters of feminist issues, and introduces five feminist values that are most relevant to the challenges of people working together.

DEFINING FEMINISM

Before we can understand how feminism contributes to business, we're challenged to develop a common understanding of what feminism is. That's harder than you might think, because it requires us to look at the world from an entirely different direction, to reconsider the nature of reality, to accept the ubiquity of diversity and the absence of objectivity, and to recognize and name the ways that conventional worldviews are designed to hurt some people and privilege others.

It's difficult work, with a valuable payoff:

Once you learn to look at the business world through a feminist lens, everything you think you should do and that you might do to grow your people and your business will change. You'll never be able to un-see oppression, and you'll never again be able to accept the status quo as "good enough," much less as "good," period. You'll no longer feel tempted to sit back and let others take up the challenge of advocating for justice, or leave it to others to envision and lead us towards a future where everyone flourishes.

Unfolding a working definition of feminism

Let's start with a definition of feminism, and then step back to consider what this definition means in full.

The simplest definition of feminism comes from the scholar bell hooks (2000, p. 1), who writes "Feminism is a movement to end sexism, sexist exploitation, and oppression." To this, I add: feminism seeks to establish political, social, and economic equality among women, men, and all people, and feminism aims to create a world where people flourish.

Feminism is a movement to:

- *End* sexism, sexist exploitation, and all oppression,
- *Establish* political, social, and economic equality, and
- *Create* a world where all people flourish.

To achieve these goals, feminism uses an array of tactics to reshape how we think about the world. For example:

- Feminism asserts that women, men, and *all* people should have equal agency, equal outcomes, equal rights, equal opportunities, equal access, equal influence, and ultimately equal and full personhood, so that everyone can participate in and shape our world.
- Feminism advocates the social, political, and economic equality of women, men, and all people, seeking equality among women and between women, men, and all human groups.
- Feminism values women and females, values the characteristics and abilities that have been labeled "feminine" and assigned to women, and values the work that has traditionally been associated with and assigned to women.
- Feminism imagines a world where the values, characteristics, and opportunities once ascribed to one gender or another are available to any person, regardless of gender.
- Feminism recognizes that current social, political, and economic systems hurt men as well as women, and it seeks the liberation of women along with the liberation of men and all people.
- Feminism emphasizes community, growth in connection, care, power through and in relationships, participation, democracy, and wholeheartedness, as well as individuals' autonomy over their own selves and decisions.

- Feminism interrogates our beliefs about what is normal, what is right, and what is desirable, recognizing that too many of our current beliefs are built on a worldview that sees women, the feminine, the physical, the natural, and the emotional as secondary to the male, while the masculine, the cognitive, the built, and the logical are asserted to be more important.
- Feminism takes a unique position on how humans should be understood, how humans should work together, and how humans should produce the goods, services, and values that support lives and communities.

As a worldview, feminism is normative, because it asserts and clarifies how the world "ought to be," and political, because it advocates we should govern, lead, manage, and organize our world around feminist values to achieve flourishing for all living things.

Feminism starts with "equality for women"

If you ask a random person on the street what feminism is, they'll likely tell you it means "equality for women." Usually, they are imagining women being equal to men, with no differences in the political and social rights, opportunities, access to resources, and autonomy of women and men. Through feminist action, and over time, what starts as an unequal status of men over women would even out as the status of women is improved. (Achieving this equality would require men to relinquish their power over women, although men's responsibility to do so is seldom mentioned when the average person talks about "equality"). In this scenario, feminism achieves its goal when men and women have equality.

Aiming to be equal to men isn't as simple as it sounds. A male standard assumes that there are no significant differences in rights, opportunities, and personhood among men. It assumes a generically privileged man, and ignores the very real disparities between different groups of men (e.g., gay men, disabled men, White men, poor men, etc.). Because we live in a world where ongoing racism, classism, imperialism, and other forms of oppression create disparities between groups of people, there is no generically privileged man to serve as a standard.

In truth, when people think about equality between men and women, they're usually implicitly comparing women and men within the same social category, for example, by comparing upper-middle class men to upper-middle class women. Racism, classism, and other systems are hard at work diverting our attention away from other differences between groups of women and men, so that we don't even recognize that we're using a standard of equality that still permits inequality (see Box 1.1 for a discussion of how equality, parity, equity, and justice are different goals on the path towards eliminating oppression).

Feminism also means "equality among women"

Another way to think about "equality for women" is to look away from the assumption that the goal is becoming equal to men, and think about women becoming equal among themselves. Equality for women means equality among different groups of women, such as among women with different religions, among women with different nationalities, sexual orientations, gender expressions, and more.

In this scenario, feminist activism would raise up women of different groups until all women, regardless of their other social categories, had equal access to opportunities, resources, and rights.

"Nobody's free until everybody's free."

Fannie Lou Hammer (1971)

By definition, feminism incorporates all anti-oppression movements, because women in different groups face different combinations of oppressions that all must be challenged to achieve equality. For women to be equal to each other, women must work for each other's freedom. Working for one's own freedom against the form of oppression that's most salient to the individual is necessary, but it is not sufficient. As Audre Lorde (2007, 138), echoing Fannie Lou Hammer (1971), explains: "There is no thing as a single issue struggle, because we do not live single-issue lives." Feminism is a collective movement, not only because feminism emphasizes interdependence and community, but also because feminists recognize they must address all forms of oppression to gain equality among women and people. Suggesting that feminism attends only to the needs of women, and not all people, is one way that the status quo has helped to turn some people away from feminism.

Combining these two standards of equality

If we put the two standards of equality together – equality among women, and equality between women and men – we'd have a scenario where women, men, and all people, regardless of their other social category memberships, all have the same rights, access, and outcomes. All have equal humanity and personhood.

That's starting to look a little better, right? This definition of feminism is more inclusive, and it recognizes that group-based differences in rights, access, and outcomes need to be addressed if we hope to liberate women and all people.

But what if I tell you that, for feminists, equality just isn't enough? This standard still puts a limit on how high the quality of human life can go. The very idea of bringing all women and men up to the same standard as societally privileged men rests on two additional, problematic assumptions. First, it assumes that what these men have achieved is what women and all people want. There's no place in this definition for women and others to create expectations and standards from their own visions. Second, it assumes that privileged men have already imagined the most fulfilling standard of human life. If they haven't, aiming for the same status as privileged men might be shooting a little low. Thus, feminists aren't interested in getting everyone equal access to what privileged men have. Feminists believe there is more that humans can strive for, together.

Box 1.1 DISTINGUISHING BETWEEN PARITY, EQUALITY, EQUITY, AND JUSTICE

Feminists, as well as businesses trying to address the unequal experiences of male and female employees, use several different terms to describe their goals. These terms – parity, equality, equity, and justice – differ in subtle and important ways related to their historical contexts and the worldviews they convey.

Parity: Parity is the goal of achieving the same proportions of women and men throughout an organization. It often refers to achieving the same percentage of women in leadership as women entering the company. For example, if the company is 25% women, then parity would suggest that 25% of managers would be women. If there were equal numbers of female and male managers, but 25% female employees and 75% male employees, there would be a bias towards women in management. As a matter of justice and representation, parity can be an important interim goal on the way to 50/50 representation of women and men.

Equality: Equality is the goal of recognizing all people as having the same value and importance, deserving the same respect, and deserving the same level of positive outcomes.

The concept of equality is often split into three pieces: (1) equality of outcomes; (2) equality of value; and (3) equality of treatment. In a worldview that promotes ideas of meritocracy and individual effort and believes that systems are free of bias (e.g., neoliberalism), the goal of equal outcomes is a non-starter. Unequal outcomes are expected simply because people have unequal merit and put in unequal effort.

Feminists' original calls for "equality for women" were calls for an equality of value. These calls challenged the legal and social understanding of women as second-class humans who were incapable of making decisions for themselves and therefore needed men to decide for them. Equality for women meant understanding women to be as fully human as men, and thus of equal value.

More recently, the term equality has been used to refer to treating men and women the same. The initial claim of equal human value was reduced to calls for "equal treatment under the law," which was further twisted to argue that everyone should experience the same process, regardless of whether or not this equal treatment led to equal or unequal outcomes for women and men, or treated women and men as equally valued human beings. Consider that if women were treated the same as men, women could not be protected from pregnancy discrimination, because men don't get protected from pregnancy discrimination. But surely, protection from pregnancy discrimination is important to valuing women as highly as men.

By diminishing the common understanding of equality down to simply and only equal treatment, anti-feminist forces gave themselves room to argue that if everyone gets the same treatment, sexism no longer exists. However, treating people the same ignores the reality that in this culture, men are assigned more value than women. Treating women and men the same ignores any need to address deficits or privileges that being devalued or overvalued might already have caused. Equality of treatment presumes that women, men, and all human beings start from the same place, need the same things, and are assigned the same value, which is not the case. To treat everyone as equally valuable, given the differences in their starting places, their challenges, and their pathways, we need to practice equity.

Equity: Equity is the process of matching the specific needs and obstacles of each group with the amount and type of support they need, so that all groups achieve the same quality of positive outcomes despite different treatment. Calls for equity assume, however, that all human beings are already understood to be of equal value. If all humans were equally valued, no one would blanch at the idea that some humans might need more or less to flourish, because it would be understood that every person's life matters equally and deserves support.

To distinguish between practices that reflect equality of value, equality of treatment, and equity, you'll hear people say "Equality (of treatment) is giving everyone a shoe. Equity is giving everyone a shoe that fits." Equality of value means that everyone deserves a shoe that fits.

Justice: Justice is the process of addressing the obstacles in the way of some groups and removing them so that the path is clear for every group, as well as removing positive bias (e.g., privilege) offered to some groups so that no group gets a head start. Justice is a more normatively loaded word than equality or equity, because it is usually invoked in contexts where there's been previous injustice and harm and/or where privilege has been aggressively denied. In a system that is just, each group has received what that group needs, because humans in all groups are equally valued. In a system that is just, the causes of earlier inequities and inequalities have been dismantled. Justice also refers to the practice of exercising neutrality, meaning that both the positive bias working in favor of privileged groups and the negative bias working against previously marginalized groups have been eliminated. When justice prevails, everyone wins.

Flourishing: the goal of feminism

You might be surprised to learn that feminist activism doesn't stop at "equality" or "ending oppression," but instead goes further. Feminism's goal is to create a world where everyone has what they need to flourish (Nussbaum, 2011; Cuomo, 1997). Being released from oppression is not the same thing as being truly liberated. To be liberated, people must have access to positive social, economic, and political conditions and resources that will give them the freedom to experience, pursue, and achieve well-being. When feminists ask what positive liberty might look like and what people free from oppression might seek, the answer is human flourishing (Harvey, 2016).

Flourishing is the individual and community experience of physical, psychological, social, economic, political, and ecological thriving. Like the definitions of "flourishing" in the fields of sustainability and positive psychology (e.g., Keyes and Haidt, 2002), feminism's conceptualizations of flourishing draw on Aristotelian notions of eudemonia (human well-being). Eudemonia is living a good, fully human life. To achieve this, flourishing requires attention to both ends and means, and both outcomes and processes, so that daily experiences as well as lifetime outcomes are positive.

Feminism envisions a world where all human beings and communities experience justice, equality, and freedom. Fully liberated people pursue self-advancement and growth while developing communities that reflect their collective values. Fully liberated people provision for themselves and others in ways that are socially, financially, and environmentally sustainable, and they attend to the flourishing of other living things and the planet itself.

Feminism leads with a critique of sexism and patriarchy

Feminism challenges sexism and patriarchy. Sexism is the collection of beliefs that privilege and value men over women, male over female, and masculine over feminine. Sexism drives behaviors, attitudes, interpretations, and priorities, and it provides institutions and society with a rationale for discriminating against women.

Patriarchy is the set of social, political, and economic systems and structures that privilege men over women, male over female, and masculine over feminine. The word patriarchy literally means "rule by the father." Within patriarchal systems, males have more rights than others, males normally hold positions of power over women, and what is seen as socially normal, desirable, and good is what is best for and determined by men. Women and others are consigned to supporting, complementary, and marginal roles, rather than central ones. Patriarchal systems are centered on men, providing what men need and want.

Patriarchy is also an ideology that promotes men's power over women, and in so doing promotes the legitimacy of power without consent. It infects everything that women and men experience, socially, economically, and at work. Patriarchy makes claims, promotes norms, and proscribes behaviors that keep women and all marginal people under the dominion of the ruling group of men. As an ideology, patriarchy works to mislead women about the reality of their lives – about how their social, economic, personal, and political positions have come about, how their roles have evolved, and even how their situation compares to the situation of privileged men. Patriarchy hides the real truth – that women and men are equally human, but that men have too long had control over women without women's clear, authentic consent.

As ideas and as conceptual models of human systems, sexism and patriarchy are so tightly intertwined and mutually dependent (and the terms are so often used interchangeably) that they are hard to treat as separate constructs. But to put it in simple terms, sexism is a set of beliefs, and patriarchy is a set of social structures built on, demonstrating, and reinforcing these beliefs about men's rightful dominion over women.

Feminism addresses all systems of oppression

Feminism relies on an analysis of gendered power dynamics to crack open a space for insight and change. But, because liberation for women and all people can only be achieved by eliminating all other oppressive systems of power, feminism incorporates not only anti-sexist but also anti-racist, anti-classist, anti-imperialist, and other movements aimed at any kind of oppression, to liberate all people equally.

Folks are often surprised to realize that feminism by definition automatically incorporates other anti-oppression movements. Something about the name "feminism" and the focus on liberating women, combined with the ways that every system of oppression works to make its machinations invisible, leads people to continue to forget that women have class, ability, religious, national, and other differences that shape their experiences of oppression and their paths towards equality and justice. Feminism has always argued that all women have some experience of patriarchy regardless of their racioethnicity, age, class, location, etc. But, some naïve feminist efforts to work for "all women" have too often suppressed or erased vital recognition of differences across class, race, ethnicity, sexual orientation, and more. This has led to mono-focused activism that treats sexism as the only relevant cause of women's oppression, and in so doing reinforces other forms of oppression.

Privileged (White) advocates of feminism, under the influence of racism, classism, and other systems of oppression and without a sophisticated understanding of feminism, have overgeneralized from their own experiences and presumed that what was important to women like them was universal to all women. For example, middle-class white women focused on managerial careers might argue "women should lean in" (Sandberg, 2013) even though for many women corporate careers are not their priority. Access to healthcare or life-sustaining wages might be more important to them.

Increasingly, feminists have pushed each other to become more inclusive and more analytically sophisticated. This has meant spotlighting the critiques of feminist women of color and anti-colonialist scholars who have called attention to their specific groups' specific oppressions and their own definitions of feminism, and challenged feminist conversation to incorporate the voices of women "at the margins" rather than "centering" feminism on white majority women's experiences. They have led feminist conversations to develop critical concepts like intersectionality, standpoint, kyriarchy, dismantling privilege, and coalition-building (e.g., Yuval-Davis, 1997).

Since the beginnings of the feminist movement, it has been challenging to teach individuals that it's the interaction of many systems of oppression, not just sexism and patriarchy, that create inequality between women, men, and all people. This challenge has led feminists to emphasize coalition-building, alliance-building, and coordinated efforts that support each other's primary and extended initiatives. Feminists recognize that it's important for each group of women (especially marginalized and previously silenced groups) to speak their truths and be heard affirmatively by other groups. Particularly important is to avoid the idea that one form of oppression or one line of activism should dominate any other.

The transitive property of oppression

Anything related to the oppression of people, to eliminating unearned privilege, and to envisioning a future where everyone flourishes is a feminist issue. It's not just because women and/or females make up at least half of any group of humans affected by these tasks, but also because none of these tasks can be achieved without working for the political, social, and economic equality of women and all people.

When some people consider issues to be simply anti-racist issues, or anti-capitalist issues, or anti-colonialist issues, and not feminist issues, they are using the same broken single-dimension approach to defining issues that is used to categorize oppressions. No issue is only anti-racist, no issue is only a women's issue. An issue might be primarily an issue of race, for example, if the group most directly harmed or to be benefited are people of color. But that doesn't mean that class, sexual orientation, employment status, or gender are not also important.

All anti-oppression, pro-flourishing issues are feminist, but they don't have to be labeled as such for feminists to feel responsible for addressing these issues. Even when gender or women aren't the primary or named axes of difference or oppression on a given issue, imagining that such an issue is not feminist contradicts feminism's broad anti-oppression agenda and also mis-recognizes the responsibility of feminists to address the issue. We can't separate racist issues from gender issues, or class issues from race issues, or capitalist issues from gender issues. It is the transitive property of oppression.

Feminism is protective and constructive

Feminism has two overarching concerns: protecting women from harm and creating a future where everyone flourishes. Feminism's protective force defends women and people who are being hurt within patriarchy, by sexism, misogyny, and oppressions of every kind. Feminism's constructive force offers a vision of the future supported by feminist values, a future without oppressions where humanity flourishes.

Protective feminism

Feminism historically has emphasized protecting, defending, and advocating for the rights of women and all people, because we live in a world where women are consistently, ubiquitously, and universally threatened. Feminism and feminists are often characterized as being angry and defensive – which makes sense, since everyone should be angry about the abuse and oppression of any human beings. Eliminating gendered and other oppressions has been feminism's most critical task, because no one can flourish when anyone is hurting.

Protective feminism has had to prove, time and again, that gendered inequality is real, that gendered inequality hurts women specifically, that gendered inequality also hurts men, and that we should fix gendered inequality and all forms of inequality. It has described the reality of women's lived experiences, as well as the lived experiences of all people suffering under systems that oppress them. Protective feminism examines how the world is conventionally "understood," reveals whose interests this understanding serves (and how), and exposes how the social, political, and economic world is organized in ways that suppress women's autonomy, women's concerns, and women's authority.

To defend women and all oppressed people, feminism has confronted not only individuals' beliefs and practices, but also family expectations, community expectations, political beliefs, cultural norms, business practices, and core-deep social assumptions. Everywhere, feminism has challenged and changed people's beliefs about what women are naturally able to do, what women are capable of, and what women want. For example, feminists have had to prove that women can do math as well as men, that women can drive cars when there's a full moon, and that women can parent effectively without male partners.

In the workplace, protective feminism has challenged conventional behaviors, relationships, practices and organizational norms and pushed to change them, to expand what people believe women and men can contribute, how work should be managed, how different kinds of work should be valued, and how women employees and leaders can be developed, recognized, and supported.

In the political realm, feminism has advocated for new laws, new legal procedures, and even new areas for legal attention to recognize barriers to women's equality at work.

Feminism's advocates have done all this within a culture that works overtime to deny and frustrate feminist progress. Feminism's progress has been hampered, to put it lightly, by the efforts of patriarchy to deny feminism's validity. Patriarchy is sneaky and shape-shifty, adapting itself whenever it can to co-opt the feminist message and keep women and people from dismantling systems of oppression. Patriarchy has even adapted and developed new ways to oppress women. For example, when laws were changed to allow women to get mortgages without a male co-signer, the rates for women's mortgages were set higher than those for men's (Kendig, 1973).

Directed at business, feminism's efforts to protect and defend the safety, the rights, and the full personhood of women and all people have helped women earn wages, keep their jobs throughout their pregnancies, have bathrooms to use, and experience a measure of physical safety in the workplace. Feminism's protective efforts have been critical for helping women (and men) survive in work organizations. But as we dismantle oppression, what do we build in its place? How do we create new systems that will elevate everyone to flourishing?

Constructive feminism

This is where the second force of feminism steps in. New strategies for moving forward come from feminism's often-overlooked second goal: to envision and create a world where all people flourish. I call this optimistic, creative, future-looking feminism "constructive feminism."

Constructive feminism is imaginative and generative – it helps us create new ideas and new forms of interaction that we haven't had before. This is critically important, because it is so difficult to imagine a world not only without oppression, but also with systems that support flourishing for all. That's without even knowing or agreeing on how we'll get there. Thus, constructive feminism helps us "build the bridge as we walk on it," by putting feminist values into practice as we build new systems. In this way, constructive feminism is "prefigurative," striving to reflect the future it seeks to build.

Constructive feminism has shaped feminist businesses such as the feminist bookstore network (Hogan, 2016) and sex-positive retail industry (Comella, 2017), as well as feminist commercial enterprises such as organic cheese-makers, green and fair trade clothing manufacturers, and software development collectives. Constructive feminism has supported the emergence of worker-owned cooperatives, the creation of democratic decision-making tools for virtual companies, and on-site childcare for employed parents. Balancing commercial demands with their own collective creativity, entrepreneurial feminists have used constructive feminism to create products and organizations that demonstrate and promote what feminists value (Orser and Elliot, 2015; Harquail, 2017). For example, feminist employees at Etsy crafted a parental leave plan that incorporated the physical, emotional, and family needs of mothers, as well as fathers, co-parents, and adoptive parents. The Gladstone Hotel in Toronto rewrote its Human Resources policies to reflect feminist values. These businesses have used constructive feminism to build processes and structures that help people flourish at work.

Transforming the system

Constructive feminism imagines not only a different future, but also ways to change systems of oppression now to help move us towards that future. Many feminist initiatives combine both protective and constructive feminism. They highlight what's wrong and also suggest ideas for what could be. In the workplace, for example, feminists want to end wage discrimination where women are paid less than men for the same jobs. They fight for comparable worth, so that jobs that are conventionally devalued because they are female, or feminine, or require "soft skills" (e.g., childcare, marketing) will be paid at the same rate as jobs of similar difficulty that are assigned to men (e.g., kindergarten teachers paid as much as garbage haulers). They rally for life-sustaining wages for all hourly workers. And beyond fixing these problems, feminists also propose creative alternatives for financial compensation to be attached to work, such as through stock grants to every employee when qualitative targets are met.

Constructive feminism promotes a shared set of inclusive values that all feminist constituencies can draw on to envision a radically different social, political, and economic future. Applied to business, constructive feminism knits together the single-themed initiatives of progressive management (such as sustainability, total quality, open books transparency, employee ownership) and returns them to their feminist movement roots and politics. Constructive feminism allows us to consider alternatives to the interwoven systems of gendered, racialized, extractive, hyper-competitive, and commercialized oppression at the core of our current economy, and offers a way to develop a comprehensive agenda for business systems change. Constructive feminism helps us imagine a world of mutuality and concern for one another in the workplace, in business, and everywhere.

Constructive feminism's core values for business

Open up a book about any political framework, be it libertarianism, conservatism, or just plain neoliberalism, and the author will start off by summarizing global and abstract principles that define that perspective. He – and it's always a he – will propose these universal, global, and abstract values like "freedom" and "liberty." Then he will come to a full stop, as though these abstractions are all it takes to capture the fundamental truths of this point of view. No-one needs these principles to be defined for them, or to have the value of these principles be proven. A simple declaration of abstract principles, by some person with authority, is all that's needed.

If only feminism worked that way. If there were an official Feminist Authority, a star chamber of experts who'd tell us, definitively, what feminism is and what feminists believe, it would be much easier to proceed with creating shared visions of the future of business. But feminism doesn't rest on objective authority. To define what is feminist lies within us as individuals and groups, since we're each responsible for identifying, learning about, discussing, and together establishing the principles that we believe guide our feminist actions. These beliefs are what I identify as "first principles" of feminism (Harquail, 2017). As first principles, these values are understood to be true and don't need to be proven.

To clarify a small set of feminist values particularly relevant to working together, I reviewed research on feminist businesses and organizations (e.g., Ferree and Martin, 1995; Ferguson, 1984) for discussions of the values that guided them, looking especially for lists created by groups of feminists. I found in Susan Koen's (1985) dissertation, for example, a list of feminist values that was generated by a group of feminists in four different work organizations. This list highlighted self-definition, creativity, and mutuality in relationships. I drew on Martin's (1990) recap of what defines feminist organizations, which highlights values like empowerment, personal growth, social relationships, service, nurturance, and mutual caring. I also drew on research in feminist design and computing for values especially related to how work should get done. From over two dozen significant texts on feminism and organizations, I gathered values that reflected centuries-long conversations about what matters to (Western) feminists working together and creating livelihoods.

I clustered and condensed these ideas into five principles:

Equality: we accord all people, regardless of their specific features, the same value, rights, autonomy, responsibility, and opportunity.

Agency: we assert that human beings can determine their own actions as they represent themselves, care for others, and change the world around them.

Whole Humanness: we acknowledge and encourage the qualities of, and differences in, human beings' bodies, minds, hearts, relationships, cycles, and development.

Interindependence: we believe that individuals depend on strong communities and communities depend on strong individuals, and neither can succeed without the other. There is no community without the individual, no individual without the community.

Generativity: we support the human need to create, to create conditions that invite growth, and to care for things outside ourselves.

Understanding the core values

It should come as no surprise that Equality is the first value listed, despite all the values being equally important. Everyday, person-on-the-street understandings of feminism focus on the principle that women, men, and all people are equally human, equally important, and equally capable. Equality also means that people of different races, ages, nationalities, sexual orientations, physical abilities, or other social categories are all equal to each other, from the beginning. Although equality is the feminist value that everyone is quick to identify, it is only half of the molecule at the core of feminism.

The way hydrogen and oxygen are tied to each other, both necessary for water, Equality is inextricably linked to a second feminist value: freedom from oppression. Casting this value in the positive sense, we call this Agency. Agency is the positive experience of freedom from oppression and the ability to take action, to decide one's own fate, and to influence the world. Equality and Agency are bonded together, because we can't be equal to one another if some of us have power over others of us. We must be able to direct our thoughts, our behaviors, our decisions, our priorities, and our goals. And we must freely choose when, and if, we will submit to the direction of another person or group.

A third value is Whole Humanness. Each person is to be valued for all that they are. All of the elements that make us human need to be respected, engaged, and cared for in our collective work of earning a livelihood. We don't believe that some parts of our humanity are more valuable than other parts (e.g., our thoughts are not more important than our feelings).

When we think of Whole Humanness, we think about all versions of human bodies as being equal – the egg and the sperm both mattering, the male and the female and the non-binary all mattering, the taller and the shorter both matter-ing. All parts of our bodies are valuable, since brains are no more necessary to our bodies than are our hearts. Relatedly, bodily weaknesses don't make anyone less deserving of empathy and care, or the chance to earn a living doing mean-ingful work. Whole Humanness reminds us of the abilities and the constraints of our bodies, such as our need for rest as well as action, drink as well as food, caring for our bodies as well as pressing them to perform. We think about our human bodies as having cycles of sleep and wakefulness, high energy and rest, attention and distraction.

Whole Humanness includes respecting our bodies and their role in recreating our species. We have cycles of fertility, raging and subsiding hormones, birth and death, and bodies that are postpartum and lactating. We are sexual beings, with and without life-mates and families. Whole Humanness embraces the different social roles that are part of being human, as well as our social responsibilities to care for each other. Whole Humanness recognizes that, as human beings, we depend on other people at the start and the end of our physical lives, to produce other living creatures, and to work together to get things done. These cyclical, biological, human elements need to be respected and cared for as we work together.

A fourth value, Interindependence, acknowledges that to be fully human (to stay alive!), we must be independent enough to care for ourselves, while also depending on and contributing to the care of other people. Physically, emotionally, and mentally, we need healthy relationships with other people so we can give, take, and share in ways that recognize each person's equal value, each person's wholeness and uniqueness, each person's gifts, and each person's human needs. Interindependence means being capable of doing things on one's own, being able to receive help from others, and contributing to the community for the good of the whole. Interindependence recognizes that we must also care for the living system that connects us all.

The fifth value, Generativity, invites us to create things that were not there before, to care about ourselves and others, to nurture opportunities and other people, and to be expressive and creative. Caring for the future, caring for non-human living creatures, caring for the ecosystem, and caring for the planet are all part of Generativity. Feminists value Generativity because we recognize that if we are to create new things and help things grow, we need to give them care, support, energy, attention, and time. Being generative is a way we become fully human ourselves.

In truth, it's not just Equality and Agency that are inseparable. Generativity makes interindependence possible, for example, since we become independent contributors after being cared for and taught by others. Each of these five values supports the others, none can exist by itself, and all are critical. As a system of values, these are connected to a larger web of feminist values that are also important to feminist visioning, but that, for now, we'll hold outside the conversation about business and management.

When we start from the premise that all people are equally valuable as human beings, that all of us have agency to act and shape our lives, that each of us needs to remain wholly human beings, that we are interindependent because we depend on each other even as we are responsible for ourselves, and that we all must care, contribute, and create in meaningful ways, we begin to think differently about how to organize ourselves to accomplish together what we can't accomplish alone. We see ourselves and our relationships creating peer-to-peer networks rather than status pyramids. We see ourselves in conversations where we can each make a contribution, where each voice matters, and where we each have a right to decide. We see ourselves doing work that fits with our bodies' capabilities, and in larger patterns and rhythms that allow for productivity and restoration, for growth as well as performance. We see the possibility of work that not only makes what we need, but lets us work together in ways that reflect what we value.

HOW FEMINISTS SEE THE WORLD: TRUTH, KNOWLEDGE, AND OBJECTIVITY

Feminism is a comprehensive ideology that contemplates ideas at every level of analysis, from the micro-level of individual biology and psychology to the meta-level of epistemology and how we as human beings verify truth and develop knowledge about our world. Feminism is universally applicable, because patriarchy is everywhere in our understanding of ourselves as a human species. Although many people assume that feminism is just relevant to relationships between women and men, or concerned about how women are treated, feminism critiques everything about our social world that supports the dynamics of domination and oppression. Feminism is not only about toxic femininity, rape culture, and the wage gap, it's also about science, morality, truth, and what it means to be human.

Stepping back and looking at the beliefs organizing our social world, feminism identifies two ideological systems at work: feminism and its contradiction, patriarchy. Feminism recognizes that while patriarchy currently dominates how people understand their lives, feminism offers a compelling alternative with a more hopeful and inclusive view. While, for example, patriarchy tells wives that their careers are less important than their husbands', feminism tells women and men that careers and family are both important for human flourishing. These two views have different definitions of truth, different requirements for assessing truth, and different understandings of how we come to believe what is true.

Feminist perspectives on objectivity and truth

Feminist scientists and philosophers challenge the notion that there is an "objective" truth, a universal truth that has a neutral point of view. The idea that there is an objective truth, one and only one way of understanding "reality" that stands apart from any person's point of view or opinion, is a core assumption of Western thinking. Objective truths are true anywhere, regardless of who is assessing reality, or why they are determining what is true. So Western scientists claim.

Feminists see things differently. Every person's assessment of reality is inextricably influenced by their position in the world (Collins, 1990). Bias, perspective, and point of view are unavoidable. Further, neither research scientists nor political theorists – nor business people – can detach themselves from the values, interests, and emotions related to their social positions, and presume that these would not influence how they ask questions, how they interpret data, and how they define social or economic priorities. All knowledge has a perspective, no matter how much it hopes and tries to distance itself from that perspective.

Feminist scholars point out how, in Western thinking, privileged men have positioned their particular perspective and their group's interests as if these were universal. Scientific methods and the hypotheses they cast have been constructed to uphold the power structures of dominant social groups. The truth they purport to validate is not universally applicable, but instead offers "distorted and partial accounts of nature's regularities and underlying causal tendencies" (Harding, 2004, 26). For example, theories of moral development, supposedly applicable to any human, were developed through studies of young white American boys and treated as universal truth. Measured by this scale, American women were found to struggle with moral development. Subsequently, research revealed that this theory described American men well, but did not fit American women or people in other cultures (Edwards, 1986). Asserting that features of a particular group of men are universal "truths" has routinely led to women and other marginalized people being "scientifically" determined to be less than White Western men.

One task of feminist scientists and philosophers has been to point out how the notion that there is an "objective" point of view is instead a falsehood imposed by the group in power. Not only is this "objective" viewpoint not neutral, but also it specifically privileges and serves the interests of the group in power themselves.

Supporting the (false) notion of an impartial, objective truth is a White Western epistemology that also pretends to be neutral, to show no preference for one group of humans or another. But both the definition of what is true and the process by which this definition is legitimated and validated are controlled by the group in power and serve the interests of that dominant group. This means that questions about what counts as knowledge – especially about people and human social systems – along with questions about what should be studied, what counts as accurate information, how data should be interpreted, and how knowledge will be used, all serve the interests of the PowersThatBe. By design, knowledge and claims of truth are relative, biased, and partial, designed to sustain the position of one group of people over others.

Feminists argue that an epistemology that promotes the idea of an objective truth is really an epistemology that's hiding whose interests it serves. They call into question the content of what currently passes as truth and simultaneously challenge the process used to arrive at these truths.

Questions about truth and reality may seem abstract or overly philosophical, until you think about the topics studied by management scientists, and the truths they promote about how to run a business or how to grow an economy. Consider that the dominant measure of national productivity, the GDP (Gross Domestic Product), excludes the economic value of work done in the home (e.g., childcare, cooking, shopping) and excludes the economic value of natural resources (Waring, 1988). Because the critical contribution of domestic work usually done by women is missing from assessments of national productivity, the GDP misdirects economic analyses and government stimulus efforts.

Feminism challenges meta epistemology

Feminism challenges the universal truths of Western thinking by denying the very possibility of "objectivity." Feminist scholars point out that Western science's methodologies are designed to help researchers and thinkers present themselves as though they were divorced from their cultural and personal points of view, as well as the values, interests, and emotions related to their material and social positions (Harding, 2004; Collins, 1990). Because these strategies for developing knowledge ask us to estrange ourselves from our human experience, these strategies contradict the value of whole humanness. Feminists propose an alternative: instead of denying the impact of one's material situation, cultural history, and standpoint, feminists argue we should acknowledge it, and then embrace it.

Knowledge from a standpoint

Feminism calls for everyone to recognize that every view of how the world works is based on some group's unique social position and material experience. Feminist scholars use the concept of "standpoint" to explain how each group and each person has their own truth, and their own perspective, based on their location and life.

To understand how standpoints work, imagine a person standing somewhere specific in the world, like Vancouver. To her north is Whistler and to her east is Toronto. Her friend in Toronto, also standing somewhere specific on this earth, has a different view. To her north is Muscoka and to her east is Montreal. Each person's view is true. Yet, what's true for the person in Vancouver is not true for the person in Toronto. Neither of these is the correct, universal, unbiased, objective view. That point of view doesn't exist.

Feminists also point out that when powerful, privileged men announce that Gatineau is up and Ottawa is to the right, they, too, are seeing the world from a specific standpoint. Although they present themselves as having unique access to "the" truth, they are standing in a specific place, and they are seeing the world from that place. Their view is no more objective than anyone else's. What they have going for them, though, is that their truths are backed up by a "hegemonic ideology." An ideology is a belief system that promotes a particular social order as the way the world is and should be. An ideology is hegemonic when it has disproportionate influence over society, so that groups submit to it even though the ideology works against their best interests. Hegemonic ideologies like patriarchy systematically conceal the ways that they support the subordination, exploitation, and domination of some groups for the benefit of the group in power. Thus, men and not women become managers of billion-dollar stock portfolios that invest in banks run by men, because women and men are taught to believe that women aren't as good with math and finance as men.

Moreover, ideologies present a view of how the world "is" – as though these arrangements were natural, normal, common, and value-neutral, when they are not. This makes the "truths" seem immune to change and foolish to challenge, even when subordinated group members are aware that what they are told doesn't ring true to their own experience. Since women naturally aren't good at math, there's no reason they should expect to manage stock portfolios or investments themselves. Women can, however, be very effective administrative assistants.

Local, authentic truths from an acknowledged standpoint

Recognizing the politics behind claims to a universal truth, feminists argue that we should draw on our life wisdom to establish our own local, authentic truths. These truths are not unsubstantiated opinions pulled out of thin air, but instead are positions developed by reflecting on and analyzing one's group history and lived experience. The stories, experiments, specific situations, local contexts, and analyses of ground-level reality together compose the truth of people's experience and their understanding of what is and what should be. Lived experience provides data that helps a group establish its own local truth that is authentic to their experience at their standpoint.

Lived experience also helps groups establish the authority to challenge the universal truths promoted by the group in power. While under the influence of a hegemonic ideology that works against their group's interests, people experience "internalized oppression" or "false consciousness" (David, 2013). But as they reflect on their lived experience and establish local, authentic truths, groups can begin to see the gap between the reality presented by the dominant ideology and the reality they experience themselves. They are able to criticize these universal "truths" as representations of a certain group's own interests, and advance their own worldview to represent the truth as they experience it. Men might claim that their organization manages diversity very well, and that despite having equal opportunities for advancement women don't get promoted because women lack career ambition. Some women might believe this, while other women check that "truth" against their own realities. They know from their lived experience that they and their female colleagues have performed to high standards. They have presented themselves for promotions only to be passed over as a white man is selected. They can confidently question the veracity of men's "truth" that their company manages diversity well, and propose a valid alternative analysis that their company discriminates against women managers.

Critical consciousness

When members of a subordinated group become aware of the gap between the hegemonic ideology and their own lived truths, and then attribute this gap to the dominant group's ideology, they begin to develop a critical consciousness (Freire, 1970). They are aware of the reasons behind these gaps, and how the dominant group benefits by making their truths seem universal. Critical consciousness also enables people to take action against the oppressive elements in their lives. As individual women, men, and people develop their own critical consciousness about how sexism and patriarchy have constrained how they see the world, they realize they can revise how they and others understand the workplace and business. They can analyze situations and propose action steps that more accurately represent their own truths and promote their own interests. Thus, the specific experiences of women, and of any marginalized group, become critically important if we are to understand a social situation and build a path towards flourishing.

The challenge for feminism, then, begins with helping women and all people come to critical consciousness about what is in their best interests, individually and collectively. This means each community needs to define itself on its own terms, to decide its own truths and its own priorities, and then craft a community, society, economy, and governance that fits its values.

Feminist interventions in business conversations must challenge "the truth" about who women are and what women want in business, about how business and the economy work, and more. Feminist interventions must expose how these truths promote the interests of privileged men, especially business owners and elite management, while they disenfranchise women and others. Feminists bring in women's voices to show that the "truth" promoted by conventional business perspectives ignores women's interests and distorts the experiences of women and all people to present them in false ways. Part of this distortion process includes misrepresenting and diminishing feminist arguments, as well as depoliticizing, selectively adopting, and colonizing pieces of feminist ideas so that they can be used to support the dominant ideology.

Feminists argue that women and all people marginalized in the workplace deserve to define and assert their own truths and visions for how to work together. This is the challenge we take up in Chapter 2 as we consider efforts towards gender equality in business, and in Chapter 3 as we discuss specific management topics from a feminist perspective.

HOW FEMINISM UNDERSTANDS OPPRESSION, PRIVILEGE, AND DOMINATION

There's no legitimate reason that men should have power over women, or that any group of people should have power over all other groups of people. People only accept this situation because patriarchy and all other systems of oppression have worked their twisted magic to make domination seem normal and unquestionable.

From bodies to domination: the "story" of sexism and patriarchy

The ideology of patriarchy builds a case that men should have power over women by telling a story that stretches from claims about the physical bodies of males and females all the way to claims about which human social qualities have more value than others. None of the claims are true. Instead, patriarchy is more like a story, a fiction with a consistent narrative arc across all cultures and times that builds the argument that men should dominate women. The story begins like this:

Step 1: biology and binary thinking

In the beginning, patriarchy asserts that there are two and only two kinds of normal human bodies: "male" and "female." Male bodies have XY chromosomes, penises, and sperm, while female bodies have XX chromosomes, uteruses, and eggs. One of each kind of body is needed to create human offspring to perpetuate the species. Simple enough.

Of course, it isn't true that normal human bodies only come in Male and Female. For instance, some people are born with three X chromosomes, or have both testes and vaginas. So, the very first move in the story of patriarchy is false. Still, the pseudo-scientific, purportedly objective "binary thinking" that divides humans into male and female not only makes two sexes different, it also makes them opposite (each has what the other lacks) and complementary (together, they have everything that's needed to make another human).

With biology supposedly having created two different kinds of bodies, society then takes over the job of explaining how these two kinds of bodies are different and related, and why these differences and relationships matter. Patriarchy tells us that male bodies create "men," who have one set of behavioral and personal characteristics, and that female bodies create "women," who have a different set of behavioral and personal characteristics. Again, they're opposites, and complementary.

Step 2: gendering

Gendering is the process of deciding which bodies should be assigned certain behavioral and social characteristics. We use the terms "masculine" and "feminine" to label the sets of characteristics, values, and meanings that are ascribed to people categorized as men and women. In a gender system, women have feminine characteristics that are supposedly tied to their biological femaleness, while men have masculine characteristics tied to their biological maleness. A few of these are idealized physical characteristics related to xx and xy chromosomes (e.g., hairy chests for males, larger breasts for females), which helps to convince people that other gendered characteristics are also related to physical bodies. Gendering then assigns to females and males ways of thinking, feeling, and behaving that are typed as "feminine" and "masculine."

Table 1.1 includes characteristics that have been defined in Western culture as being typical for males and females. Notice how each feature in the Feminine column is matched by its opposite in the Masculine column. The opposites are

Table 1.1 Masculine and Feminine Characteristics

Feminine Characteristics	Masculine Characteristics
Dependent	Independent
Submissive	Dominant
Passive	Active
Emotional	Rational
Intuitive	Logical
Responsive	Commanding
Gentle	Tough
Weak	Strong
Obliging	Aggressive
Home-oriented	Worldly
Sensitive	Hardy
Warm	Cool
Nurturing	Demanding
Indecisive	Decisive
Kind	Firm
Seeks security	Seeks adventure
Persuasive	Commanding

also complementary, so that strength is balanced by gentleness. These sets of characteristics are drawn as though there were no third or fourth option, and as though a single person couldn't have qualities from both columns.

Gender as a performance

Living up to the expectations of one's assigned gender is a complex task, although we often take this task for granted because gendered expectations and gendered performances start even before a person is born. In feminist circles, you'll often hear gender described as being a "performance" (Butler, 1990), as something people *do* rather than *are*. When people are "doing gender" (West & Zimmerman, 1987), they are behaving in ways that reflect, demonstrate, and continue to create the expectations of their gender, as it is defined in their particular culture. Gender performance can also include having the appropriate physical type and bodily characteristics, some of which can be changed simply by behaving differently (e.g., changing a haircut, dressing in pants or skirts) and some of which are more difficult to revise.

Through repeated acts in everyday situations, women and men demonstrate and are seen by others as having certain gendered perspectives, qualities, and behaviors. These behaviors are not related to biology; instead, they are cultural patterns determined by patriarchy. Gender performance and gendered behavior are regulated, policed, and reproduced in our society by the power structures associated with patriarchy. "Men" and "women" are socialized into appropriate gender roles and performances, so that they learn and internalize socially expected and acceptable masculine or feminine traits and behaviors and are rewarded for gender-appropriate behavior.

Note, though, that not every person displays these characteristics appropriately or lives up to the standards of masculinity and femininity. How well a person performs these roles often influences how well they are accepted in society (e.g., "girly men" are often ridiculed, as are "tomboys").

Gendering is culturally specific and historically contingent

What's considered feminine in one culture may be masculine in another. For example, in Russia, male ballet dancers are masculine, while in the United States, boys who do ballet are oftentimes bullied for being effeminate. Even Table 1.1 earlier is specific to one culture. These masculine and feminine characteristics are typical, not of men and women universally, but specifically of White, European men and White, European women. These qualities do not map neatly onto what's considered masculine and feminine in African-American culture, not only because African-American and White European American cultures are different, but also because in a racist society, White femininity is defined against African-American femininity. For example, while White Anglo-Saxon women are feminine if they are ornamental and fragile, African-American women are feminine (or most womanly) when they are strong and competent.

Gendering specifics can also shift over time. One hundred years ago, pink was preferred for boys because it was a stronger color. Blue was recommended for girls because it was more delicate and daintier. Yet by the 1940s, these color recommendations had reversed (Paoletti, 2012), because in truth these associations were arbitrary.

Our ideas about what's masculine and feminine are ever-changing, but what appears consistent is this recurring pattern: patriarchy asserts that when something is characterized as feminine, it has less value. And, when something has less value, it's seen as feminine.

Gendering is oppositional and hierarchical

Not only are masculinity and femininity opposites and complementary, they are also organized in a hierarchy. What is thought to be male, masculine, and of men is seen as superior to what is female, feminine, and of women (to reflect the ways that patriarchy ties bodies, qualities, and identity together, I use the terms male/masculine/men and female/feminine/women to indicate when a phenomenon can't be anchored to just one of these three features).

This does not mean that masculine characteristics and men are indeed superior to feminine characteristics and women; rather, it's that patriarchy has determined that the specific characteristics associated with masculinity in our culture are valued above those associated with femininity. For example, in Western White culture, we tend to value strength over weakness. We value being rational over being emotional. We value independence over dependence, competition over collaboration. The second characteristic in each pair, the feminine and less-valued one, inherits its value largely from its ability to complement, balance out, or otherwise flatter the preferred masculine characteristic.

Much of what's constructed as femininity such as being sensitive to other's feelings, or being cooperative, or preferring to share power, can also be understood as behaviors people develop when they are subordinated. Servants learn to intuit the needs of their masters, prisoners learn to work together to educate themselves on their legal rights, and so on. Femininity can rightly be understood as the coping behaviors of female subordination in an oppressive system. More simply, femininity is the performance of qualities that a culture expects of women, rather than qualities that are inherent in and authentic to any woman's personality.

Step 3: essentializing: bodies cause differences

Once the story of gender separates human characteristics into two distinct halves and assigns men and women each their own colors, patriarchy moves on to Step 3: essentializing.

Essentializing is the process of asserting and believing that the differences between how women and men think, feel, and behave are caused by differences in female and male bodies. Thus, Western women are talkative because they have vaginas, and gentle because they have ovaries. Meanwhile, Western men are decisive because their brains are typically bigger, and they are demanding because they have hairy chests. That's how the logic of essentializing works. People essentialize women when they assume that girls and women are *naturally* emotional, nurturing, docile, weak, vain, dependent, and so on, precisely because of their female bodies.

To be sure, there are some hormonal, neurological, and biological differences between male and female bodies that seem to be linked to differences in behavioral characteristics and cognitive qualities. For example, high levels of testosterone make men (and women, and all people) more physically aggressive. While many sex-related social differences have been found, nearly as many have been debunked by less biased follow-up scientific studies. Yet even where biological differences exist, their social impact is usually insignificant (Hyde, 1981). In other words, nurture and socialization largely override hormones.

Linking personality and aptitude to bodies is a great way to legitimize different social positions for men and women. After all, if your brain is smaller because you are female, there's no way you can become an effective Prime Minister or CEO. And, if you're sensitive to others' feelings because you have a uterus, you might be better off in marketing or HR where feelings are helpful, rather than in finance or manufacturing where feelings are irrelevant. But, of course, neither cognitive abilities nor personal qualities are the automatic or inevitable result of biology.

The key problem with essentializing – besides it being untrue – is that essentializing limits the possibilities for any group of humans. It locks us into gendered roles and gendered expectations, and locks us out of opportunities to grow and fully develop all of our abilities. With essentializing, one's body becomes a permanent form of containment and limitation.

That's why essentialism plays a very special role in transphobia and discrimination against trans people and gender non-conforming people. For example, if the social characteristics that define one's gender are based in one's body, how can anyone "be" a gender that's different from the one anchored in their body?

Box 1.2   WHO IS INCLUDED IN FEMINISM'S DEFINITION OF "WOMEN"?

"One is not born, but rather becomes, woman." With Simone de Beauvoir's (2011, 283) most famous pronouncement, she recognized how females' bodies are only loosely related to the achievement of "woman-ness."

The idea of "women" and "men," two groups of human beings defined by having female or male bodies is a social construction, a categorization scheme that our culture uses to organize how we collectively see the world. "Women" and "men" are also political designations, because these social constructions reflect who's in charge and thus who gets to set, use, and benefit from distinctions made between people. The label "women" is applied to some humans and not others, and is used to put them into a group whose capability, authority, and destiny can be determined by the group "men."

There is an ongoing discussion over who can consider herself a "woman" and be part of the group for whom feminism advocates (cf., Serrano, 2010), as well as part of the group that is explicitly targeted by sexism and misogyny, and so on (e.g., Zack, 2005). Therefore, if we understand that "woman" is a political category and not an objective biological category, it helps us see that there are several criteria – some biological, some relational, some social, some even arbitrary – that are used to sort humans into the political class of "women" to be subordinated by men.

Feminists want people to have the authority to define themselves rather than to have political identities imposed upon them. When we recognize Women as a political category, we can welcome in anyone who experiences the world as a woman or as a female, and ask them to work together to liberate all women and people. Then we'd call them feminists, too.

Step 4: male dominance: patriarchy

This final step in this story of patriarchy is that the beliefs, expectations, behaviors, and values attached to male and female, masculine and feminine, and men and women, get codified into norms, rules, and systems of culture and organization. For example, the gendered expectation that women are more nurturing leads society and women themselves to expect that women will be better at nursing than men but, oddly, not better at being doctors. Women are better at caring for and teaching children than men, while men are seen as better at building technology or running governments. The full array of how we do things and the broad spectrum of beliefs about why things are as they are supports gendered differences, the power and value differences connected to gender, and the roles assigned to women and men. Patriarchy as a system enshrines and automates the domination of all things male/masculine over all other things female/feminine.

With this story, patriarchy builds a rationale for men's domination of women as a group, and then uses this rationale to design the structures that shape the ways we learn, work, play, govern, and live.

Patriarchy as a structure of male privilege

Patriarchy, like any structure of privilege, is organized around three basic principles: dominance, identification, and centeredness (Johnson, 1997). First, it is dominated by men. The default is for all positions of power to be occupied by men, or by non-men who act just like men. Male dominance doesn't mean that every man is powerful, but rather that most who are powerful are men.

Cultures that are male dominant use men/males as the standard for understanding and supporting human beings in general. The business term "manning the controls" defines the human capacity for driving machinery as a male feature, even though women, men, and all people can easily turn knobs on a dashboard.

Male-centeredness puts masculine perspectives at the center of the culture's world view. In centering maleness, patriarchy also pushes femininity to the margins, positioning femininity/females/women as less important. When one category of people is set as the standard for human beings in general, we presume that somehow that group is superior. In male-centered systems, whatever men do is not only the standard, but is also better. For example, unbroken career paths that men can pursue are considered better than the fractured career paths pursued by women who interrupt paid work – however briefly – to give birth. Male identification encourages men to understand women as different to and less than men while remaining unaware of their own male privilege.

Some people misunderstand patriarchy and think that it is about the individual behaviors of individual men. They think that discrimination via patriarchy must occur through individuals' intentional behavior. Rather, because patriarchy is encoded into public policies, institutional practices, and cultural norms and then rationalized by patriarchal ideology, our behaviors and beliefs are conditioned to maintain the power dynamics that sustain that hierarchy, privilege, and subordination, unless we intentionally intervene to change these structures (Johnson, 1997).

Sexism as foundation and model for all other oppressions

Some feminists have argued that sexism is the primal form of oppression in humanity. Andrea Dworkin argued long ago that "(S)exism is the foundation on which all tyranny is built. Every social form of hierarchy and abuse is modeled on male-over-female domination" (1976, 68). It's true that sexism is a form of oppression that subordinates over half of human beings. And, it's true that analyses of gendered dominance help us understand how other systems of domination are constructed. However, as feminism has developed a more sophisticated understanding of the oppression of women as a class, it's become clear that focusing only on gender as an analytic category won't fix the whole situation. Remember that a gender-only equality does nothing to eliminate differences between groups of women and thus doesn't achieve equality among women or between women and men and all people.

Sexism is a single axis of oppression

Sexism is now commonly understood as one "axis of oppression," a single dimension on which some people are oppressed and others are privileged. On this axis, men are at one end with relative power and privilege, and women are at the opposite end with less power and less privilege. However, sexism is not the only system of oppression that affects women and other people. There are many forms of oppression, each represented by its own axis, that hold down some groups of people while elevating others.

When discussing oppression, people tend to forget that categories like gender, or race, or sexual orientation are social constructions – they are ideas and labels and categorization schemes that we use not only to cluster people into groups, but also as heuristic tools we can use to analyze society. Heuristic tools cut through complex situations by identifying distinct aspects to focus on and explain, while pushing other aspects into the background. Heuristics offer us imperfect, yet useful, insights. Dimensions of gender, or class, or sexual orientation help us focus on one reason at a time to explain oppression and domination that is in fact created by system of interlocking dimensions too complex to tease apart.

Multiple oppressions contribute to women's inequality

Black feminist scholars, in their quest to call attention to the qualitatively distinct oppression that Black women face due to racism and sexism, developed several constructs to overcome the simplification caused by analyzing women's oppression only on the basis of gender. These concepts include intersectionality (Crenshaw, 1989) and the matrix of oppression (Collins, 1990).

Critical race theorist and law professor Kimberlé Crenshaw (1989) focused feminism's attention on the oversimplification of a gender-only approach when she proposed the term "intersectionality." Using the heuristic metaphor of two different roadways that intersect, she described Black women's lives as being subject to two forms of oppression at once, creating a qualitatively different experience of oppression for Black women when compared to both the sexism experienced by White women and the racism experienced by Black men.

Crenshaw demonstrated how American case law, by applying a single dimension of oppression at a time, left out the experiences of women of color. Gender discrimination could not explain why Black women experienced different expressions of sexism than White women, while racial discrimination could not make sense of different experiences of racism experienced by Black women but not Black men. The specific experiences of Black women disappeared, because in both gender and racial discrimination cases Black women were the less privileged group and not the implicit focus of the analysis. These single-category analyses made Black women's specific oppression legally invisible even as Black women lived this experience every day. More than one, and even more than two, dimensions of difference are needed simultaneously to understand each group's qualitatively unique experience of oppression as the result of multiple power hierarchies.

Patricia Hill Collins, a Black feminist philosopher of science, offered a different heuristic for managing the complexity of oppressions. Collins imagined several individual axes, each sorting people towards one or the other end of the axis, so that part of the group dominates and the other part is subordinated. For example, on the racism axis, Whites are privileged and people of color are oppressed. She proposed that these axes intersect and tangle with each other to form a macro-system of oppressions she labeled the "Matrix of Domination" (Collins, 1990).

To envision how these different axes of oppression work at the same time, imagine them as spokes in a wheel, where each dimension is a spoke that passes through a shared center where all the spokes intersect. This cross-section view makes it easier to see that on each axis, part of each group is benefiting from the other part's oppression. The cross-section also shows us something about the force that is opposite to oppression. The opposite of oppression is not "freedom" or "equality", it is unearned privilege. Since the privilege that men receive via sexism comes at the expense of women and the privilege that white women receive via racism comes at the expense of Black women, feminism must challenge all unearned privilege to move towards freedom and flourishing.

Kyriarchy, the matrix of domination

The all-encompassing web of oppressive systems, this matrix of domination, has another name: kyriarchy. Kyriarchy, a neologism coined by theologian Elisabeth

Schussler Fiorenza (1993) means "rule of the masters." Going beyond patriarchy's "rule of the fathers," kyriarchy recognizes all kinds of power-holders, focusing us on the idea that there are many stories about who should have dominion over whom, and why. These systems reinforce each other because they all support the same core idea: that one kind of person, one category of person, should have dominion and power over all the others.

While the word kyriarchy may seem awkward, there are good reasons to know and use the term. First, "kyriarchy" helps us promote the understanding that what is holding down women and all people isn't just patriarchy. Indeed, for some women and people, patriarchy and gendered oppression feel less of a priority than economic oppression, or racism, or religious discrimination. Kyriarchy reminds us that feminism needs to challenge all forms of domination.

Second, many people get confused by the word and concept of patriarchy. They think that patriarchy is only about "sex" and "gender" dynamics and they fail to recognize the underlying power story that patriarchy tells – that male/masculine/men get to have power, without the consent of those over whom they have power. It's necessary to emphasize that what's going on with patriarchy has less to do with gender than with one group asserting power over another – just as racism has less to do with race than with one group asserting power over another, and just as heterosexism has less to do with sexual orientation than with one group asserting power over another. Every story about oppression and privilege, regardless of the dimension of oppression, makes the same moves: there are two groups (us and them) who are different. We are better, they are "less than," we deserve to dominate them. End of story.

Moving forward

Now equipped with a working definition of feminism, a sense of feminism's protective and constructive concerns, and five feminist values for business, you understand more of what feminism is. You can appreciate how and why feminism challenges the acceptance of an objective worldview that's used to silence women and feminism's advocates. You can see past the fiction of gendering and recognize it as a common trope for legitimating the idea that some people should have power over others by virtue of their social category memberships. And you can affirm why feminism takes responsibility for addressing all forms of oppression.

By responding to feminism's first intervention and learning from the voices and experiences of women and feminism's advocates, you should now be able to deploy feminism to analyze and reimagine social, economic, and political practices. You should be capable of assessing the breadth and depth of the changes that are necessary to propel business and all social systems towards justice. This should help you make the most of Chapter 2, where we will consider the second of feminism's interventions: advocating for gender, racial, class, and all forms of equality in business, so that business practice reflects and advances justice.

Just as important, though, is that you should be ready to explore creative ways to practice a new form of business, one that helps build our paths into a future where everyone flourishes, where businesses make important and useful things, where individuals work in meaningful jobs for wages that reflect the value they create, and where all of us work to live rather than live to work, in communities and ecosystems that thrive because they regenerate us.

QUESTIONS

1. How has considering the revised definition of feminism and the five feminist values changed your expectations about how feminism can be relevant to business?
2. Why have we seen so much of feminism's protective energy and relatively little of feminism's constructive energy?
3. Where do you see the different steps in the story of gendering play out in the workplace?
4. What do you think of the feminist argument that gendering is really a strategy for establishing the power of one group over another?

Mini Box: privilege, defined

Privilege is a set of unearned assets and benefits given to people who fit into social groups on the dominating end of an axis of oppression. These group privileges give some people preferential treatment as well as institutional power over members of other groups. These privileges also allow some groups of people to be relatively unburdened by the oppressions of a particular organization or culture. As with oppressions, the privilege each person experiences are qualitatively different from what other people experience based on the unique combinations of social groups that people are part of.

REFERENCES

Butler, J., 1990. *Gender Trouble: Feminism and the Subversion of Identity*. London, Routledge.

Collins, P.H., 1990. *Black Feminist Thought: Knowledge, Consciousness and the Politics of Empowerment*. New York, Routledge.

Comella, L., 2017. *Vibrator Nation: How Feminist Sex-Toy Stores Changed the Business of Pleasure*. Durham, NC, Duke University Press.

Crenshaw, K., 1989. 'Demarginalizing the Intersection of Race and Sex: A Black Feminist Critique of Antidiscrimination Doctrine, Feminist Theory and Antiracist Politics'. *University of Chicago Legal Forum*: 1989, Article 8.

Cuomo, C.J., 1997. *Feminism and Ecological Communities: An Ethic of Flourishing*. New York, Routledge.

David, E.J.R. ed., 2013. *Internalized Oppression: The Psychology of Marginalized Groups*. New York, Springer.

de Beauvoir, S., 1948. *The Second Sex*, translation by C. Borde and S. Malovany-Chevallier, 2011. New York, Vintage.

Dworkin, A., 1976. *Our Blood: Prophecies and Discourses on Sexual Politics*. New York, Harper & Row.

Edwards, C.P., 1986. 'Cross-Cultural Research on Kohlberg's Stages: The Basis for Consensus'. In: S. Modgil and C. Modgil, ed., *Lawrence Kohlberg, Consensus and Controversy*. London, Routledge, pp. 419–430.

Ferguson, K.E., 1984. *The Feminist Case Against Bureaucracy*. Philadelphia, PA, Temple University Press.

Ferree, M.M. and Martin, P.Y., 1995. *Feminist Organizations: Harvest of the New Women's Movement*. Philadelphia, PA, Temple University Press.

Fiorenza, E.S., 1993. *But She Said: Feminist Practices of Biblical Interpretation*. Boston, MA, Beacon Press.

Freire, P., 1970. *Pedagogy of the Oppressed, 30th Anniversary Ed.*, 2006. New York, Continuum.

Hammer, F.L., 1971. Speech Delivered at the Founding of the National Women's Political Caucus, Washington D.C., July 10 1971.

Harding, S.G., 2004. *The Feminist Standpoint Theory Reader: Intellectual and Political Controversies*. New York, Routledge.

Harquail, C.V., 2017. Clarifying Feminist Values for Business. Available at: www.cvharquail.com/feminist-business-tools/values/. Accessed: October 16 2018.

Harvey, C.D., 2016. 'Nature, Feminism, and Flourishing: Human Nature and the Feminist Ethics of Flourishing'. Unpublished Ph.D. dissertation, Marquette University, Milwaukee, WI.

Hogan, K., 2016. *The Feminist Bookstore Movement: Lesbian Antiracism and Feminist Accountability*. Durham, NC, Duke University Press.

hooks, b., 2000. *Feminism Is for Everybody: Passionate Politics*. New York, South End Press.

Hyde, J.S., 1981. 'How Large Are Cognitive Gender Differences? A Meta-Analysis using w^2 and d'. *American Psychologist*, 36(8), pp. 892–901.

Johnson, A.G., 1997. *The Gender Knot: Unraveling Our Patriarchal Legacy*. Philadelphia, PA, Temple University Press.

Kendig, D., 1973. 'Discrimination Against Women in Home Mortgage Financing'. *Yale Review of Law & Social Action*, 3(2), pp. 1–15.

Keyes, C.L.M. and Haidt, J., 2002. *Flourishing: Positive Psychology and the Life Well-Lived*. Washington, DC, American Psychological Association.

Koen, S., 1985. 'Feminist Workplaces: Alternative Models for the Organization of Work'. Unpublished Ph.D. dissertation, Union Graduate School, The Union for Experimenting Colleges and Universities, Cincinnati, OH.

Lorde, A., 2007. *Sister Outsider: Essays and Speeches*. New York, Ten Speed Press.

Martin, P.Y., 1990. 'Rethinking Feminist Organizations'. *Gender & Society*, 4(2), pp. 182–206.

Nussbaum, M., 2011. *Creating Capabilities: The Human Development Approach*. Cambridge, MA, Belknap Press.

Orser, B. and Elliot, C., 2015. *Feminine Capital: Unlocking the Power of Women Entrepreneurs*. Redwood City, CA, Stanford Business Books.

Paoletti, J.B., 2012. *Pink and Blue: Telling the Boys from the Girls in America*. Bloomington, IN, Indiana University Press.

Sandberg, S., 2013. *Lean in: Women, Work, and the Will to Lead.* New York, Knopf.

Serano, J. 2010. *Whipping Girl.* Berkely, CA, Seal Press.

Waring, M., 1988. *If Women Counted: A New Feminist Economics.* New York, Harper & Row.

West, C. and Zimmerman, D.H., 1987. 'Doing Gender'. *Gender & Society*, 1(2), pp. 125–151.

Yuval-Davis, N., 1997. *Gender and Nation.* Thousand Oaks CA, Sage.

Zack, N., 2005. *Inclusive Feminism: A Third Wave Theory of Women's Commonality.* Lanham, MD, Rowman & Littlefield.

2

OBSTACLES AND APPROACHES TO GENDER EQUALITY IN BUSINESS

INTRODUCTION

The primer on feminism in Chapter 1, "A primer on feminism for business: Defining feminism," demonstrated the first parry of feminist interventions: bringing forward the voices of women to broaden the way we all understand the world. The primer describes feminism's values and goals while explaining how feminism challenges domination and the gendering that supports domination. With this foundation, we now turn to the second parry of feminist interventions: challenging gender inequality in business organizations.

Gender inequality in business has been hard to challenge. Despite lengthy and well-intentioned work by companies and individuals within companies, efforts to eliminate gender inequality in businesses have had only limited success. For organizations and individuals who want to challenge gender inequality, there are three obstacles to their efforts.

First, a neoliberal belief system defines the appropriate role of business and keeps us from using business as an agent of change in our personal, social, and political worlds. We live in a culture that celebrates business as a positive force and looks to business for new ideas. We believe that modern business thinking will get us the enhanced economic performance our culture seeks, and yet we don't even think about aiming for flourishing through business.

Second, a postfeminist attitude suggests we've made enough progress towards gender equality and makes it hard to justify or even consider feminist interventions in a business.

Third, the presumed gender neutrality of businesses tells us that sexism exists outside the magic circle and appears when it is brought in by members. In fact, rather than being neutral contexts, businesses themselves are active participants in re-creating and sustaining gendered inequality in complex ways that are hard for lay people to appreciate.

Together, these three sets of obstacles have diverted, contorted, and even blocked the routes that individual women and organizations have thought might get us to gender equality in business.

OBSTACLES TO GENDER EQUALITY: NEOLIBERALISM, POSTFEMINISM, AND GENDER STRUCTURE

Neoliberalism

Just as fish don't think about the water making them wet, most people don't think about the ways that their belief systems influence how they interpret the world around them. But all of us have belief systems, like monotheism or veganism, that influence how we understand the world. These belief systems exist in our perceptual background, often without us recognizing them or analyzing them, making us wet when we aren't even aware of the water itself. The way we comprehend the world simply seems to be the way the world "is." Right now, many business students and business people, along with much of society at large, find themselves submerged in a belief system that shapes how we understand the role of business in society: neoliberalism.

Neoliberalism is the contemporary political perspective that dominates every conversation you'll ever engage in regarding business, the economy, government, and international politics, without you even realizing it. Because of its dominance, neoliberalism also influences how we think about the relationship between feminism and business, and even how we understand the challenges facing feminism itself.

Neoliberalism (like feminism) is a political ideology, a way of understanding, organizing, and imagining how we should govern our world, from international markets all the way down to how an individual understands herself and her life options. Neoliberalism is an opinion about the proper role of politics and a theory about economic policies, enmeshed with each other. Even the name of the early American instantiation of neoliberalism – "Reaganomics" – is a mashup of political and economic terminology. "Neoliberalism" itself is a contested term, but is generally understood to be a perspective on governance that seeks to expand the use of market mechanisms, imagery, and priorities into every corner of human life. It is a philosophy that privileges markets and market logic over democratic processes and human rights. In this way, neoliberalism profoundly contradicts feminism's emphasis on community and fully human (not market) agency.

The policies promoted by neoliberalism depend on the assumption that "free markets" and the protection of private property will inspire individuals to be entrepreneurial and take responsibility for themselves, leading to their individual well-being. Neoliberal beliefs undergird processes like privatizing government and social services, reducing the number and scope of social and welfare provisions, deregulating businesses and individual behavior, and retracting the role of the democratic state. Instead of promoting collective, political, and democratic decision-making, neoliberalism idealizes buying, selling, pricing, and profiting. Ultimately, neoliberalism "reduces every aspect of human experience – from love, to labor, to the human body – to its capacity to create profit" (Hills, 2014).

More market

Neoliberalism pushes for the expansion of "market logic" and economic thinking beyond the business context and into all areas of political and social life. The neoliberal response to every social problem or question is "more market." Because democratic control by citizens is "inefficient," public services like schools and water systems should be turned over to for-profit corporations who can run them more productively, using the supposedly superior logics, tools, and priorities of businesses. Thus, businesses' criteria are used instead of citizens' criteria to decide what should be done, and how, on behalf of the public and society as a whole.

Less government, less community

Neoliberalism argues that government regulation and oversight, whether over the financial sector, the environment, or drug manufacturers, distort markets' efficiencies. Regulation is considered unnecessary, because all that's needed to keep pollution, exploitation, usury, or any other ill in check is "more market." By reducing regulation that protects individuals and non-corporate entities or offering tax breaks for the rich and corporations, for example, neoliberalism privileges for-profit companies and their owners while reducing support to citizens and communities. Without any government assistance, people are expected to "pull themselves up by the bootstraps" by participating more efficiently in the workforce and by making better personal choices.

Instead of a national government that cares for the health of citizens (e.g., schooling, infrastructure), neoliberalism pushes towards privatizing the ways these basic needs are met, to make them the responsibility of each person or family unit, while reducing the role of community and the common good. Consumers' independent action and choices are emphasized over community decision-making. Overall, by shifting as much as possible away from democratic government processes to market-based, profit-oriented processes, neoliberalism seeks to maximize individual private abundance for some over the collective, public abundance of everyone.

Celebrating *Homo economicus*

Neoliberalism takes as its unit of analysis the lone individual. Neoliberalism assumes that people will act like the efficient, utility-seeking hero of every Economics 101 class: Homo economicus. Making relentlessly good choices with unimpeachable rationality, Homo economicus maximizes his own self-interest within the competitive marketplace, leading to his well-being. Note that this rational actor is a true abstraction. He is untethered from class, race, and cultural standpoints that might influence his choices.

The collateral effects of his self-maximizing behavior on other people and on the concept of a "public good" are not discussed in Economics 101. In the world of Homo economicus, you won't find a community to take into consideration. Similarly, there are no collective interests that differ from his own or which might influence how this rational actor makes his decisions, governs himself, or considers the needs of others. He simply doesn't care about others or the community. Nor will you find a conversation about how or why this actor would work collaboratively with other individuals to secure common good for others over himself. It's all about the individual rational actor, calculating his every move.

Neoliberalism insists, despite vast evidence to the contrary, that every man is an independent, rational, responsible agent. Individuals will effectively use the market to pursue and satisfy their interests. To do this well and to maximize his choices in the marketplace, each individual must become an entrepreneur of his own self. He must develop his "human capital" to be employable and even to be considered a worthy human being. And he must develop himself independently, without help from anyone and using his own bootstraps, because the shift of responsibility from government to the corporation, and from the corporation to the individual, means that each individual must put forth his own entrepreneurial labor to be an effective competitor in the marketplace. We can see the impact of the neoliberal logic in the rise of the gig economy and along with it the proliferation of for-profit businesses offering the chance for each of us to buy additional skills training. Individuals must work constantly at self-improvement, self-investment, and the efficient application of their personal human capital to maximize future returns.

There are, however, many places in social and individual life where business logic does not work. For example, I cannot calculate the return on investment of the number of hours I "spent" nursing my two children. Yet neoliberalism asks me to treat this parenting choice as some kind of rational, utility-maximizing decision, with no emotional meaning, no nurturing intent, and no contribution to the community. The business case for breastfeeding diminishes the entire experience.

To think of ourselves as businesses, we must operate ourselves, invest in ourselves, manage ourselves, and strategize over how to participate in the marketplace. We must also compete with each other for market dominance and everyday low prices, rather than help each other, care for each other, or recognize each other's equality. Thus, reduced by market logic to self-serving businesses, people no longer pay attention to notions like citizenship, duty, compassion and solidarity, much less the common good, interindependence, and generativity. There is simply no rational, profit-oriented reason to care.

Because neoliberalism promotes the idea that individual choices are the solution to problems, every problem becomes the fault of someone's previous (bad) choice. Losing a job during a recession or not being promoted to partner is not only our fault, but also our individual problem to fix. People are told to "take personal responsibility" and "make better choices" or even "lean in" to change their situations. This logic might work in a world where there are jobs to fit every person's abilities, where every full-time job earns someone a life-sustaining wage, and where any increase in effort leads to a commensurate increase in reward. That, alas, is not the world we live in.

"Business" "logic" everywhere

"If it works in business it should work everywhere else," says neoliberalism. Even for organizations that are obviously not businesses, such as non-profits and charities, neoliberalism directs managers to use business tools and thinking, as though caring for the poor were the same as caring for a fleet of buses. Both nuns and mechanics would disagree. The incursion of business thinking into other sectors might make sense if businesses indeed had tools for dealing with emotions, family relationships, and conflicts of interest in a community. Instead, businesses and market logic are often ill-equipped to handle a full range of whole human and social needs, much less to do this with democratic methods that honor different groups' priorities and agency.

And even if a business had the requisite skills, its market logic might not serve social interests very well. Neoliberalism isn't a world view that cares about justice, or even about flourishing for everyone. Its goal is to maximize the profits of private business and the elite group who own businesses, by privatizing community services, responsibilities, and relationships, and without ever addressing existing inequalities and systems of domination that place 'rational actors' at wildly different starting points within the market. In the neoliberal paradigm, "equality" is the opportunity to compete, period. Everyone is assumed to have the same bootstraps and the same ability to pull themselves up. There is no consideration of different starting points, different sets of choices, different responsibilities, or that each individual needs shoes that fit before the race even begins.

Neoliberalism goes by some other names, like "late stage consumer capitalism" and the term preferred by Pope Francis: "Savage capitalism" (Reuters, 2013). Our descent into "savage capitalism" has been marked by increasing inequality, financial and economic insecurity, social fragmentation, and constricted opportunity. Politically, savage capitalism

> has corrupted and distorted our public discourse, creating a system that is increasingly unrepresentative of, and unresponsive to, the concerns of the citizenry. It is a system that sees only private interests, locked in competition – hence, it has no vision of the common good.
>
> (Stafford, 2013)

Neoliberalism interferes with business people's efforts to see the world from the viewpoint of the community and the common good that are prioritized in feminism. It's especially difficult for business people to turn around and challenge neoliberalism with other belief systems – like feminism – that so thoroughly contradict neoliberalism. We are often too flattered by the importance neoliberalism places on business thinking and business practices (in which we ourselves as business people are deeply invested) to spend much energy paying attention to where neoliberalism goes too far, and where business thinking is ill-equipped or simply inappropriate for organizing most human relationships.

Given this recap of neoliberalism, you can anticipate the many ways that feminism and neoliberalism conflict with each other. Feminists challenge neoliberalism because it displays contempt for what feminism holds dear, especially the values of interindependence, whole humanness, agency, equality, and generativity. And, because neoliberalism is normalized and treated as inevitable, it often seems as though feminist values are irrelevant, if not impotent, in face of neoliberalism's dominance.

Postfeminism

Another belief system that obstructs efforts to advance gender equality is one that masquerades as a positive outcome of feminism itself: "postfeminism." As much as the zeitgeist of neoliberalism hampers our ability to appreciate feminism, widely held contemporary views about feminism make it difficult for people in businesses to even think the concept is necessary. Postfeminism is a sensibility, a series of claims, and set of positions about whether sexism (still) exists and whether feminism is (still) needed or useful (Gill, 2008). This cluster of cultural beliefs dominates our conversations about the status of gendered inequality, its causes, and appropriate remedies.

Why "post" feminism?

Although postfeminism is "about" feminism, it isn't a feminist perspective. This postfeminist mindset reflects both deeply rooted sexism and an incomplete understanding of feminism, and it gets in the way of understanding gendered inequality and sexism in organizations. Just as "humanism" is casually, but incorrectly, applied to the idea of "human liberation," postfeminism has taken on a meaning that seems sensible but is actually incorrect.

Take the name "post" at face value and it suggests that this conversation is what we have "after" feminism has successfully run its course. Like a postprandial digestif follows a formal dinner, a postfeminist stage might suggest a victory lap to celebrate the conclusion of the feminist movement.

But postfeminism isn't the "next" stage in the positive movement towards feminist goals. Postfeminism is a cultural response to the challenges feminism has posed and the progress feminism has made. It includes some acceptance of feminist ideals and perspectives, as well as backlash against and resistance to full gender equality and social justice. What defines postfeminism is the way that feminist and anti-feminist ideals are entangled (Gill, Kelan, and Scharff, 2017), so that people see the progress of feminism even while experiencing ongoing sexism. Most people have neither a strong understanding of how our systems continue to produce inequality nor a clear vision of a healthier system where the concerns and suggestions of feminist critique have been resolved and incorporated. Instead, we have a cultural level double bind, where "feminist ideas are both articulated and repudiated, expressed and disavowed" (Gill, 2008, p. 441). These profoundly contradictory beliefs are twisted together, making little sense and offering confusing advice. We see women aiming to be agentic and assertive, only to be criticized for being too aggressive and unfeminine. We see organizations celebrating their appointment of a female marketing director, when they have no senior women in their engineering departments and don't pay a living wage to their sales clerks. We hear contradictory claims about the progress of gender relations, what's expected of women and men, and what's expected of companies.

We also hold contradictory beliefs about the proper role of feminism. At the same time as there appears to be a resurgence of feminist activism (like the #MeToo movement), we also see heightened misogyny in popular culture (Gill, 2014). Feminism is taken for granted as being useful at the same time as it's described as being irrelevant (McRobbie, 2009). These entangled ideas and contradictions reduce our clarity around the problem of inequality and make it impossible for us to come to a consensus about a strategy for change, "leaving a landscape devoid of collective political feminism but rife with imagery of so-called female empowerment" (Monteverde, 2014).

In the confusion and contradiction, the truth is obscured. Somehow, we can't acknowledge that efforts to address gender inequality exist alongside efforts to reinforce and reproduce it. Instead, we use several postfeminist strategies to avoid making sense of these contradictions. One strategy is to treat gender inequality as something that happened in the past, but no longer happens here (Kelan, 2009). Sexism is a problem of earlier generations and older cohorts that is disappearing over time as younger, newer, and more enlightened cohorts enter, says a white paper by Deloitte (Smith and Turner, 2005). By linking potential inequality to a previous generation, millennials are now able to assert that they don't expect gender bias to influence their business experience or career paths.

In businesses and society, "sexism thrives in the present because it appears to dwell in the past" (Calder-Dawe, 2015, p. 89). If sexism existed in the past, then ongoing or additional anti-sexism activism and structural changes in the company really aren't necessary anymore. And, if sexism just went away as older employees aged out of the company, changes in how the company runs weren't (and still aren't) needed. Rather, equality has been achieved by attrition as the "old fogey" sexists retire. Gendered bias has literally left the building.

Another strategy for managing these contradictions is to assert that gender inequalities might exist, but in other contexts (e.g., in rap music, but not business), in other countries (e.g., in Saudi Arabia, but not here in Canada), or even just in other departments (e.g., in engineering, but not in marketing). Suggesting that we should compare our situation to others', count ourselves lucky, and then move on teaches us not to worry about or fight against the inequalities that other women and people experience since these inequalities aren't ours.

And suggesting that there's not much sexism here anymore, at least not compared to other places, urges us to accept that the sexism we feel right here and right now isn't all that bad. Apparently, a little sexism, like a little racism, is socially acceptable. Moreover, if sexism doesn't really happen in our company, when sexism does occur it must be an exception. Thus, we focus on individual bad apples like movie studio chiefs, and not the whole rotten sexist system of Hollywood. Finally, if and when sexism or male privilege is noted, it's accepted with a sigh, then dismissed as "just how workplaces are" (Gill, Kelan, and Scharff, 2017).

Postfeminism focuses on individual women's agency

Postfeminism, following the lead of the larger ethos of neoliberalism, shifts emphasis away from organizational, structural, and cultural causes of sexism to focus on the choices, behaviors, and self-understanding of individual women. Postfeminism says little about what's expected of men. Because it ignores the system-level causes of gender inequality, as well as the more subtle manifestations of patriarchy, postfeminism disingenuously claims that a woman's individual agency is the best approach for making minor necessary improvements in her work prospects.

Working women's first job is to reshape themselves to fit postfeminism's updated definition of the ideal business woman. Unlike the traditional patriarchal stereotype of women as meek, supportive, and subordinate to men, the postfeminist patriarchal stereotype presents women with a revised set of gendered expectations. Women are no longer to be seen (nor see themselves) as passive objects or as victims of gendered bias. Instead, they are expected to be active, self-defining, goal-pursuing agents. Women in postfeminism are confident, agentic, in control of their own destiny, and – dare I say it – empowered.

Women in business are told to treat themselves as products that can be branded, modified, developed, enhanced, and focused in ways that fuel their individual success and thereby contribute to the organization's success. To increase their business value, women are encouraged to improve themselves psychologically and behaviorally, to develop better and different skills, and to monitor and evaluate themselves constantly. Treating themselves like new and improved products helps women apply market logic to their own behavior and outcomes, all so they can perform up to men's standards.

Women in business must not only achieve a certain level of work performance but also must re-fashion themselves to fit into the postfeminist feminine ideal. Postfeminist business femininity is more agentic than previous versions of femininity, but it is still soft, still collaborative, still nurturing, still submissive (Gill, 2014). This updated femininity remains essentialized, attached to, and expected of a female body, but this version plays comfortably with updated forms of organizational sexism (discussed later in Chapter 3, "Feminist interventions in core business concepts").

The same "makeover culture" we see in fashion magazines that tell women to diet, exercise, wear makeup, and dress smartly pervades business culture too. Consider the mini-industry devoted to teaching women to negotiate for raises, to develop "power poses," and to close the "confidence gap" (Gill and Orgad, 2017). Because women's lack of confidence (not some kind of gender-biased culture or systems) inhibits their success, women must become more entrepreneurial, develop different leadership behaviors, dress professionally yet stylishly, use a bullet journal to make every minute productive, pursue mindfulness, and even practice "self-care" to restore and revive themselves so they can work more enthusiastically tomorrow.

Still, when postfeminism produces women who are anxious about their faults, unsure of their appropriate femininity, and working furiously to fix themselves, companies get an agentic, go-getting employee who's ready to work (and work on herself) to get ahead. Indeed, she's so busy focusing on herself as the solution that she forgets to (also) advocate to change the system. She's a reassuringly feminine go-getter who never rocks the boat, a perfect postfeminist businesswoman. Ultimately, she'll remain in her appropriate gendered position, subordinate to the powers that be.

Silencing conversation about actual sexism

Sexism in a postfeminist worldview enjoys the protection of Harry Potter's Invisibility Cloak. Tossed over endemic sexism, the Invisibility Cloak makes sexist acts, biased norms, and gendered processes disappear right in front of the everyday observer. Gaslighting people and businesses by telling them that sexism no longer exists, postfeminism makes it hard for anyone to see it. Women don't recognize when sexism is hurting them at work (Crosby, 1984). Men don't see the sexism that women experience and tend to dismiss it too (Becker and Swim, 2011). Companies don't believe they have much more to do beyond promoting a few more women. Sexism has been made to disappear.

By selectively accepting some feminist elements and simultaneously dismissing the notion of gendered bias, postfeminism not only makes sexism difficult to see, but also makes it hard to call out and contest. Women who raise concerns about sexism are pointed in the direction of a high-achieving woman and told, "She did it, why can't you?" Businesses that focus too much on gender equality are thought to be wasting their time and their shareholders' money. Token successful women and token women-positive policies serve as alibis that protect organizations against criticism as well as against deeper collective self-reflection. They are exceptions that prove the rules of the magic circle.

The co-presence of progress and resistance makes reality feel equivocal. For every instance of sexism, there's a seemingly rational, superficial, non-systemic explanation. "He's just being friendly." "She doesn't have executive presence." "Women don't really like the technological elements of engineering." Meanwhile, there is a feeling of some real progress. More companies are hiring women. Women's wages are rising. Women are CEOs, COOs, and heads of marketing.

Moreover, when we say that sexism and gender progress are both present, what's often heard is that sexism and gender progress are equally prevalent and equally powerful. They are neither. There are fewer initiatives to promote equality than there are policies and practices that reaffirm gendered inequalities (Ortlieb and Seiben, 2017). And, sexism is more powerful. It is reinforced not only by inertia and by its ubiquity, but also by the active efforts of many to sustain and even promote the idea that men/male/masculine is better than and deserves power over women/female/feminine and others (Riley, 2001).

Contributing to the silence is the problem that too many business people lack the vocabulary to articulate what they see and the analytic skills to understand where it's coming from. Without terminology like interindependence, concepts like intersectionality, or analytic tools like the matrix of oppressions to specify what's happening and understand how to dismantle gendered bias, business people experience just one random-seeming antifeminist incident or another, and not something systemic and powerful that's worth a business's attention.

Contradictory logic of organizational efforts to ease gender inequality

Organizational efforts to ease gender inequality are presented in confusing ways. Some programs are described as efforts to reduce gender bias at the same time that these programs are lauded for making good business sense. For example, a company sponsors a boot camp for women to become software developers and has first dibs on the most talented participants. What looks like affirmative action for women is just as plausibly a recruitment device to address a tight labor market. Of course, we want businesses to succeed, and we want them to become more feminist places where everyone can flourish, simultaneously. It would seem this is just what companies are doing when they launch initiatives to help women. But in most cases, it's not that a company is genuinely being feminist and promoting feminist values, but rather that the company is using just the parts of feminist ideas that have the most direct link to the business case. While this company is helping some women learn to code and perhaps become its employees, the company is also resisting deeper change and deeper engagement with feminist critique. That's not real change.

The fatigue of conflicting realities

The difficulty of reconciling conflicting realities ("Sexist bias is everywhere, hurting women!" "Gender bias is disappearing!") leads people to experience what Kelan (2009) calls gender fatigue. Gender fatigue occurs when individuals are challenged to simultaneously acknowledge that gender might play a role while insisting that it does not. People are tired of seeing gender discrimination and prefer to see a world that is already gender equal and where gender no longer matters (Kelan, 2009). Whether they retreat by saying that "sexism exists, but ... ," "it is aging out," "it happens over there," or "it isn't really relevant to my work situation," people find ways to look away from contradictions and the dissonance they cause. Looking away helps people keep sane: sexism is real, but they feel safely distanced because they refuse to see it in front of them. Refusal takes energy and makes people tired, but gets us nowhere.

In a postfeminist world, organizations also suffer from gender fatigue. They respond by highlighting all the positive work they are doing to help end gender bias, while simultaneously refusing to track the data that would alert them to the presence and breadth of inequality. For example, they count the gender ratio of job applicants, but don't analyze trends of bias in recruiting practices. Or, they retreat to tropes and clichés about what to do (fill the pipeline, empower women, celebrate diversity, etc.) even though they know these strategies are insufficient. What they don't do, alas, is use feminist concepts to understand their business or to envision its future. Nor do they reach out to feminist consultants or activists for help. Instead, businesses deploy surface-level practices that seem to promote equality, at least a little. They use postfeminism's declawed and defanged "feminism-lite."

Feminism-lite

In the marketplace of ideas, postfeminism glides its cart down the aisle of feminist critique, tossing in claims that seem sweet and tasty while bypassing critiques that are too heavy, too challenging, or frankly too threatening. In the cart goes "empower women," but left on the shelf is "challenge unearned privilege." Postfeminist sensibility judiciously selects the fun, easy, and consumerist elements of feminism and plucks them from their political critiques. In the marketplace of ideas, postfeminism sells us a hip kind of feminism exemplified by social and sexual freedom, pleasure, wages, jobs, and careers, but no politics. For women, this means the chance to prove themselves as employees, managers, and leaders and become junior partners in the status quo. For companies, it means the chance to reduce the worst of gendered inequalities (slowly, of course), to revise, update, and reform business practice, but not to transform it. Feminism-lite is powerless against dominance, male privilege, or business owners' primacy; it is unable to challenge how profits for some are prioritized over flourishing for all.

Contradictions of postfeminism in business point to deeper issues

Given the contradictions of postfeminism, shouldn't we try to resolve them? Could we tell a corrected story, a coherent story, where sexism exists alongside progress towards gender equality, but where our commitment to justice and equality, along with our understanding of feminism, helps us chart a course towards flourishing? That would not be a wrong approach, but it would only take these contradictions at face value. It's also important to understand the purpose that these contradictions serve, both in postfeminism and in neoliberalism. These contradictions serve the interests of the powers that be, those few elites in power.

Simply put, these contradictions work to protect business leaders and owners. When women are on the hook to make room for themselves, when individuals are held responsible for the impact of corporate and government decisions, and when people in power make just enough of the right kinds of adjustments to make it seem like progress is happening naturally, no one is forced to make big changes in how business is conducted or how it is understood. The contradictions of postfeminism take away the urgency for feminist action, while the individualism of neoliberalism takes away the systemic analysis and the motivation that would lead us to work together on each other's behalf.

In this way, feminist efforts to transform organizational systems and culture, much less business as an activity, or industries, or the entire economy, seem unnecessary, unrealistic, and overmuch. We just expect more hard work from each individual woman, and maybe a little adjustment from a few random "bad guys." The net result of postfeminist and neoliberal belief systems is that businesses adopt a few new buzz words. Businesses can claim to have paid attention and done their bit while turning their backs on their own culpability in supporting the deeper forces of gender inequality. Feminist efforts in businesses are no longer relevant or necessary, if they ever were. So postfeminists would have us believe.

Box 2.1   WHEN WOMEN BENEFIT FROM EQUALITY INITIATIVES

While they are working so hard to improve themselves, businesswomen who were once seen as hampered by gender bias are now often accused of benefiting from efforts to end gendered bias. That would be the point, of course, since these efforts are appropriate and equitable ways to get women shoes that fit so they can run in the same race as men. Now, though, some see women as being given an unfair head start. In the eyes of some people with a postfeminist mindset, gender bias against women has been replaced by bias against men (Gill, Kelan, and Scharff, 2017).

I occasionally hear this concern from male students, who think it's unfair when firms recruiting on campus hold special events for female job applicants, or when the university sponsors a salary negotiation workshop specifically for female business students (though male students are welcome to attend). They see the attention paid to women, but are unable to put it in its proper context, to recognize it as an effort to redress previous sexism rather than as unnecessary preferential treatment (aka positive discrimination). No one ever says, of course, that men have been advantaged by preferential treatment all along. Nor do people note that these efforts to help women haven't eliminated gender bias. (There's the contradiction again). Men seldom, if ever, understand these programs that are ostensibly to help women might also help men enjoy a workplace where meritocracy is a plausible feature and where they, too, could flourish.

Gender structure in organizations

Despite confusion over the sources of gendered inequality, the fact of it remains: women don't have full, equal participation in the workplace and in the economy. But what is business's role in sustaining gendered inequality? And what can individual companies do to achieve gender equality?

The first step in addressing these questions calls for businesses to understand how gendered inequalities are built into every level of organizations. It's easy to underestimate what this might take because there are too many ways people are discouraged from analyzing the organization itself. Three obstacles include:

1. *People assume patriarchy, sexism, and gender inequality are only about sex and gender,* and not about gender being one strategy (among many others, including racism and homophobia) for building a hierarchy of power. They focus on differences in how women and men socialize, and not on how some people assume authority over others.
2. *Most people don't think organizationally.* Outside an organizational behavior or sociology class, people are not taught about the many levels of analysis and

the interlocking dynamics that construct organizations as entities. They don't know how to think beyond individual-level phenomena.

3. *Organizational change is profoundly complex.* Businesses struggle with plain vanilla organizational change initiatives, such as those related to pursuing new strategies, adopting new technologies, and upgrading management practices. Any organizational change demands a multi-level strategy and requires members' involvement at every stage, and few managers have experience planning and participating in successful change efforts.

The framework of gender structure

Feminist sociologists, struggling to anchor the concept of patriarchy in everyday social systems like the home and the workplace, began to develop theories about how rationales supporting men's power over women were made manifest in social structures. Acker's (1990) theory of gendered organizations brought this thinking together and forward when she proposed the framework of "gender structure" to show how gender differences in organizational behavior and outcomes were best explained by structural and organizational characteristics and not just individual ones. Gender structure refers to how gendered rationales (i.e., the gender story in Chapter 1, "A primer on feminism for business: Defining Feminism") shape an organization, through five interrelated influences:

1. Individuals' own gendered identities and their ideologies about gender are expressed in their behaviors and expectations.
2. Interpersonal interactions where participants' beliefs about gender help to create patterns of dominance and subordination and establish status and marginality.
3. Group-level and organization-wide practices and routines (like the informal division of labor, recruiting practices) where beliefs about gender are used to make organizational decisions.
4. Cultural processes such as stories, symbols, and slogans that members use to describe and rationalize the divisions and hierarchies caused by gender (e.g., something as simple as an organization's slogan, like "Just do it" could convey a preference for masculinity over femininity).
5. Gendered ideology, a fully fledged world-view about how the world should be, that shapes beliefs about how the organization should be managed, including beliefs about the value of work and workers, about authority and leadership, and about right and wrong.

Beliefs supporting gendered inequality are used to shape every level of our social arrangements (Halford and Leonard, 2001).

In an important revision, Acker (2006) later expanded her conceptualization of gender structure to incorporate an intersectional analysis by integrating race, class, sexual orientation, and additional dimensions to propose the notion of "inequality regimes," an organizational structure analogous to the matrix of domination.

Building on and adjacent to Acker's framework, other feminist scholars proposed similar groupings of social mechanisms that help to build gendered evaluations and dynamics into organizational life. Together they describe what Giddens (1984) would call a social "structure" – the collective norms, processes, routines, contracts, arrangements, and so on that exist outside of individual desires and motives, and that are more than what's internalized by each individual as their guiding norms and values. Feminists argue that social structures (like organizations) become gendered because the norms, arrangements, expectations, and people that compose organizations are all gendered.

Gender structure provides many simultaneous explanations for gendered phenomena that we see in organizational practices where gender is explicitly involved (e.g., dress codes for women and men, maternity leave policies) as well as those where gender is quite active but seems to be irrelevant (e.g., job design, office space, and expense accounting policies). For example, a company may think its dress codes for women offer guidelines for looking professional, while these codes are also ways of controlling women's bodily comfort, self-expression, and sexuality (Rafaeli et al., 1997). Companies may adopt open-plan offices where everyone seems equal because they have the same desks and square footage, except that women, and not men, experience open offices as pressurized places where their appearance is constantly being evaluated (Hirst and Schwabenland, 2018).

The multi-level gender structure framework helps us appreciate why insights, programs, and changes at one level of an organization don't have the power to eliminate gender inequality generated at other levels. For example, it helps us understand why, when women and men with individual-level beliefs about gender equality come to work in organizations with gendered hierarchies of valued and less valued work, women get sorted into less valued customer care work and men into more valued technical work, ultimately reproducing gendered inequality. Even if one or two systems at one or two levels have improved and become less sexist, all the other elements of the gender structure are continuing to work at reproducing sexism and inequality.

Gendered inequality is not like a Jenga tower where you can make the whole structure collapse simply by destabilizing one dominant log. Offering parental leave doesn't fix all discrimination against mothers. Sexist processes at different levels buttress each other, holding the structure in place even while a gender equality effort makes progress on one plane. Similarly, the structural nature of gendered inequality helps explain why, even with our very best intentions as individuals and organizations, we can be re-creating gendered inequality without even wanting to.

Gender structure helps us understand how we can continue to hold contradictory beliefs about gender equality, seeing both progress and rampant sexism. At the same time that we see positive movements in one area, we can see active, negative processes in other areas. Both are true. The concept of gender structure shows that while gender inequality persists, it works in such complicated, interactive, and mutually reinforcing ways that it's difficult to pull apart, much less to knock down.

Neoliberalism focuses on individual people as problems and solutions, closing off our ability to see other sources of inequality and change energy. Postfeminism argues that sexism barely exists and that gendered inequalities are improving, so not much needs to be done. And, because we underestimate the ways in which gendered inequality is built right into business organizations, our approaches to change are too simplistic. Thus, we are confused about who is most responsible for making a change, whether much effort is needed, and what, if anything, businesses need to do.

This confusion helps to explain why organizational and individual efforts to promote gender equality have achieved only limited success. Next, we'll consider what organizations and individuals have tried to do, and what has impeded their progress.

COMMON APPROACHES TO ACHIEVING GENDER EQUALITY IN ORGANIZATIONS

At least on the surface, most people and companies seem to be fine with the idea that women who want to work for pay should have reasonable opportunities, and most businesses have embarked on programs to improve women's prospects as employees. This is itself an accomplishment for feminism. Yet while these initiatives to move towards gender equality appear to be responses to feminist arguments, none of them reflects feminism's full critique or practices feminism's constructive vision. The feminist challenge to business only starts with achieving the job opportunities, equal pay, career progress, and personal meaning that full participation in business offers to men. Still to be addressed are not only making sure women's voices are fully heard, but also bringing feminist values into our conceptualizations of business so that we can use business to help us move towards human flourishing.

Organizational approaches for gender equality

Businesses have launched any number of initiatives to resolve the problem of gender inequity. Each of these approaches has its own diagnoses of the causes of inequality and its own definition of the desired end state.

Building on the contributions of Acker (1990), Ely and Meyerson (2000), and Calás and Smircich (1996), we can describe six different approaches that organizations have taken to address gender inequality. Table 2.1 displays these approaches and the problem diagnoses, recommended action, assumptions about organizations and women, and vision of the future associated with each approach. These approaches include:

1. *"Add women and stir"*: change the number of women in business overall and in management positions by hiring more women and promoting them as they perform.
2. *"Fix the women"*: teach women to play the game, but leave the rules of the game unchanged. Because women don't know how to lead, behave, or contribute the way that the best male employees do, we can train women to do things better and improve their performance.
3. *"Value the feminine"*/value differences: capitalize on women's uniqueness and differences to men in positive ways, to take advantage of what women do well naturally.
4. *"Equalize opportunities" by fine-tuning the system*: adjust formal systems, focusing on structural barriers to women's recruitment and advancement, to make policies fair for women and men.
5. *Deep cultural change with "small wins"*: pursue change in foundational elements of the organization, focusing on projects that benefit the business as well as move towards gender equality.
6. *Transform the system to help everyone flourish*: transform business to reflect feminist values and goals, to achieve democratic organizations free of dominance and inequality where everyone flourishes while the business performs.

These approaches aren't mutually exclusive. A business might simultaneously be pursuing tactics around fixing the women, adding more women, and valuing the feminine even as they're trying to transform into a flourishing organization, and one approach often can lead to the next. All six approaches make some progress, however limited, and all of them encounter resistance and backlash.

1. "Add women and stir"

Adding women into the mix makes sense to businesses that believe there are no other gender-related issues beyond ineffective and maybe discriminatory hiring practices that have led them, historically, not to hire women. The idea of hiring more women to satisfy calls for equality assumes that these women will stay in the organization, achieving some success and getting promoted somewhere up the ladder. It also assumes that achieving a place in an organization is the same as being able to influence an organization. This approach treats women as though they are not particularly different from the men around whom the business was originally designed. Women should have no problems that would keep them from doing well in the game, especially given that the game is fairly designed to be played well by anyone.

Table 2.1 Organizational approaches to gender equality

Approach to equality	Problem diagnosis	Action	Assumptions about organization	Assumptions about women and people	Vision of organization
1. "Add women and stir"	Not enough women have been hired.	Hire more women.	Gender neutral organization welcomes all.	Women are just like men. No need for men to change.	Status quo, just with women too.
2. "Fix the women"	Women don't perform effectively.	Teach women to play, leave the rules unchanged.	Gender-neutral business will reward women commensurate to contributions.	Women are capable, but need to be more like men. No need for men to change.	Status quo, with women performing as men.
3. "Value the feminine"/value differences	Women's natural abilities have not been appreciated.	Hire women for their feminine talents, where these talents are needed.	Companies can adjust their values because they need women's qualities.	Women and men are naturally different. Women can be valuable complements to men.	Expanded status quo, with more feminine qualities and skills.
4. "Equalize opportunities" by fine-tuning the system	Formal systems have been biased against women.	Small procedural adjustments will help women assimilate.	Organization is welcoming, but needs to fix a few blind spots.	Women are as capable as men, but processes need to be fair for women and men.	Adjusted status quo. Organization is fair, with men and women experiencing no obvious gendered bias.
5. Deep cultural change with "small wins"	Organization's structure and culture sustain bias.	Pursue small changes in system, culture, and individuals simultaneously.	Focused and deep approaches will eventually spread equality throughout company.	Women and men have much to offer. Companies should help both succeed.	Company structure and culture change to become more equitable.
6. Transform the system to help everyone flourish	Organization's structure and culture sustain bias and don't address flourishing.	Pursue multiple, multi-level changes through democratic design and participation.	Business can increase performance and flourishing by ending reliance on domination.	All people can redesign and change company to achieve shared goals.	Company embodies feminist values, supports human flourishing, and achieves business success.

Adding women addresses demographic parity, not power and equality. This approach imagines equality as a numbers game, what Alvesson and Billing (2002) refer to as "body counting." A military metaphor seems apt here because so many of these new female recruits are stopped dead in their march up the ladder by land mines buried in the organization's gendered structure.

At face value, there is nothing wrong with efforts to increase the number of women by hiring more women. It has to start somewhere, right? But getting more women employed in good jobs that fit their skills, challenge them, pay them, and get their best contributions depends on more than just hiring women. It depends on making sure that there's a fit between the women-identifying people coming into the business and the work, jobs, roles, and culture they are joining.

Like drops of oil in water, which never dissolve to blend into the water no matter how much you stir, women don't blend into organizations designed for men. When all a business does is "add women and stir," without simultaneously and deliberately changing the cultural and structural elements that continue to sustain gender bias, they may achieve demographic parity, but they don't achieve gender equality.

2. "Fix the women"

When women are hired into an organization that is designed for men and where men are already performing, women struggle. Why don't women perform? Why don't women contribute? Why don't women know how to lead? Why can't women be more like men? So, the problem diagnosis changes. It's not that there aren't enough women. It's that there's something wrong with the women we've hired. They need to be fixed.

Businesses' efforts to eliminate gender inequality turn to focus on developing in the women they've hired whatever additional skills, attitudes, and behaviors they need to succeed just as men do. Women are sent to leadership development courses, classes on negotiating salaries, mentoring programs to get one-to-one targeted coaching, the whole gamut of human resources technology. With this help, women should acquire a repertoire of skills to help them perform a lot more like the men for whom the organization is really designed.

This approach assumes that since the organization is gender-neutral and fair to everyone, women will want to learn how to act just like the men who've succeeded already. Even if they do learn to act more like men, women will usually be less successful than men at acting like men (Carli and Eagly, 2007); men have had much more practice.

Efforts to "fix women" are seldom tailored to account for specific challenges that minority women might face. Every woman does the same power pose, whether she's Black or White, a first level manager or COO, in a digital startup or an investment bank. The programs are designed to meet the needs of white women who can be coached to fit more tidily into the power structure without disrupting White dominance. These technologies ignore important differences between women, such as specific context, material resources, and physical/bio-logical realities that might make it difficult for many women to execute these fixing strategies, much less succeed with them.

Moreover, these fixing programs and the type of repaired female employee they envision includes mostly managerial women because investing in the skills of managerial employees returns value to business. Meanwhile, there's no inter-est in changing the stereotypical expectations of men, to make any effort to fix the men too, or to adjust the ways that masculinity shapes jobs, roles, and per-formance expectations. For example, there will be no changes to the expectation that leaders be controlling and forceful, making it hard for men who are quiet and collaborative to fit in.

Approaches for "fixing the women" address them as individual potential per-formers, as if gender equity will be achieved by some appropriate number of successfully renovated individual women. This approach purposely leaves organ-izational policies and structures intact, so that the women who can be fixed enough to assimilate themselves can do so with minimal disruption to the status quo (Ely and Meyerson, 2000).

2.5. Fix the women and the men

A half-step up from the "fix the women" approach is one that intends to fix both women and men. It's an improved, more sophisticated, higher level of fixing, like adjusting both the seat and the handlebars of your rented bike. Women can improve their gender-specific inadequacies and both men and women can fix their more egregiously gender-biased behaviors, norms, and attitudes. Together, women and men attend diversity training, learn how to check their privilege when they conduct performance appraisals, avoid sexual harassment, and recog-nize their unconscious bias. The idea is that, if people understand what sexual harassment is, they won't do it. And, if employees discover (through a scientific, objective test) that they are actually not as race- or gender-blind as they assumed, they might confront their own biases at work.

On the plus side, this expanded fixing approach recognizes that men, as well as women and other people, need to learn how to behave differently at work in order for the organization to move forward on gender (and race and other) inequalities. On the downside, none of these individual fixes makes a big dif-ference in the overall culture and structure that reproduce gender inequality, because the multi-level gender system overrides one-shot training by reasserting the biases everywhere else in the organization. Few individuals have a mindset strong enough to resist the everyday bias-normalizing pressures of the full gen-der structure.

3. "Value the feminine"/value differences

The "value the feminine" approach, revised to "value differences" to synch up with diversity and inclusion programs, seeks to deploy conventional gendering

processes to serve the organization's needs. It sustains the binary split of qualities to either men/male/masculine or women/female/feminine, and keeps
them assigned to the bodies of men and women, respectively. It recognizes that
organizations have historically valued only the behaviors, styles, and forms of
work traditionally associated with men and masculinity, while devaluing, sup-
pressing, or otherwise ignoring those traditionally associated with women and
femininity (e.g., Kolb et al., 1998). Now, instead of businesses treating feminine
qualities as "less than" or subordinate complements to masculine ones, they
will dissolve gender inequality by ranking and valuing feminine qualities (and
women/females) as equal to masculine qualities (and men/males). Thus, valuing
the feminine leads us to celebrate gender differences and not eliminate them.

In this approach, the feminine/female qualities that were once devalued
are now prized, because they soothe and even compensate for the masculine
qualities of men. Femininity has become, for women employees, the "Female
Advantage" (Helgesen, 1995), and feminine qualities are the "Ways Women
Lead" (Rosener, 1990). For example, where global sales require the empathy and
relational dexterity demonstrated by moms and girlfriends, feminine women are
the answer. The female advantage gets played out in programs and interventions
around "gender awareness," "gender balancing," and "gender bilingualism."

Beneath this reevaluation of feminine qualities is an instrumental business
argument. Because new forms of work now require previously rejected feminine
characteristics, women become a newly valuable "human resource." Once mis-
fits, women are now "special." This approach suggests, though, that feminine
qualities and the women who bear them will be valued only to the degree that
they are useful to fix or support men. No matter how useful it is to have a lid, the
lid is never as valuable as the pot it fits.

Like the racist approach of "separate but equal," valuing the feminine ignores
the purpose of the gender binary, which is to assign status and power to one
group (men/male) over another (women/female). As long as the gender binary
is retained, so too is the power and status hierarchy it constructs. One gender
is the standard, the other gender is the compliment. The top of the binary is
never equal to the bottom. It would be a feat of social cognitive reengineering to
value feminine qualities as highly as masculine ones without liberating ourselves
from the gender binary. Sure, women get to be Heads of Human Resources, but
Chief Global Officers are still men. Even when praised and valued, stereotypical
feminine qualities still fall slightly short. And even if women's "special" qualities
are celebrated in the short-term, the assumption of difference or "otherness" of
women has a long half-life, keeping men/masculine and women/feminine seg-
regated, opposite, and unequal.

4. "Equalize the opportunities" by fine-tuning the system
"Equalizing the opportunities" shifts the emphasis away from women as the
cause of gendered problems, deficiencies, or benefits, and onto the organization

itself. Instead of fixing women, this approach wants to adjust the organization's formal systems to treat women a bit better.

The equal opportunity approach recognizes that a well-intentioned business's systems and policies can create obstacles that are harder for women than men to surmount or that challenge women alone. Businesses can adjust their rules, practices, and management systems to remove structural barriers to women's recruitment and advancement. Removing the barriers sounds dramatic, but this strategy is more about incremental adjustments to existing systems. In truth, it doesn't challenge an organization too much to pay the same wage to women and men in the same roles, or to promote women who meet their sales goals as soon as they promote the men who do. Even when it comes to making adjustments that treat women differently, such as with maternity leave for managerial mothers, these rarely require an overhaul of the organization's larger systems. Initiatives like flex-time or remote work that seem designed to help women with family responsibilities can turn out to benefit the men and the business too. More recently, we've seen programs that target specific behaviors, using data and behavioral design to reduce bias in systems (Bohnet, 2016). These include changes, like adjusting the language in job postings and evaluating resumes without gender-revealing names, that help improve the overall candidate pool and not just the number of women who are considered for a particular job. Policy-tuning makes good business sense.

These system-tuning programs can (and have been) useful in the day-to-day lives of employees. They have helped to increase the number of women in entry and middle-level positions and to a much lesser degree the CEO suite, offering role models and good company for the increasing number of female bodies in business. This approach has even helped organizations make many of the diversity gains that they celebrate right now (Smith and Turner, 2005).

What's missing is an equity approach that both eliminates group-specific barriers and supports key differences among people (Radoynovska, 2019). No amount of formal, procedural equality can achieve equality among people starting at different social places and facing different obstacles. Formal procedural equality will help, but gender inequality will still be reproduced by the gender system in other ways.

5. Deep, narrow, cultural change with "small wins"

Deep, narrow, cultural change with "small wins" approach takes a more complex perspective on gender and gendering in organizations (Ely and Meyerson, 2000; Correll, 2017). It draws on theories of gender structure to consider interventions that address many components of the gender structure simultaneously. This approach might address gender-biased behavior by individuals at the same time as addressing a larger organizational process that creates gendered inequalities. Deeper cultural work shifts the focus from fixing the women to fixing the underlying, systemic factors that lead to workplace inequity (Kolb et al., 1998).

Gendering isn't something that only women and men do; instead, it's understood that organizations create and maintain a gendered social order that prioritizes men/masculinity.

Importantly, instead of taking a multi-part, broad program of interventions across an organization, this approach targets narrower, deeper, and more local cultural changes. Change agents aim their interventions at relatively small aspects of an organization's culture that have direct implications for both gender and productivity. For example, a team might be taught to become aware of their own unconscious bias, and then redesign and bias-proof their hiring interview protocols to lock in their personal learning and change the system (Correll, 2017). The goal is to find practical, powerful, and palatable changes that can demonstrate business impact and proof of concept, paving the way for additional changes.

While the deep change with small wins approach recognizes the complexity of gendered systems, the narrowness of its scope (e.g., small, local wins) makes it hard for lessons learned to spread to other parts of the organization. It's like injecting fertilizer horizontally into the trunk of a tree. The fertilizer will nourish the area it touches directly but will take a long time to spread across the tree's trunk, and even longer to reach up to the branches and down to the roots. Still, if done repeatedly and deliberately, over time it can help the tree grow healthier.

6. Transform the system to help everyone flourish

In theory, there exists a sixth approach, where businesses transform themselves from conventional organizations structured by gendering to feminist organizations pursuing not only gender equality and social justice but also human flourishing at every level. These businesses would transition themselves from conventional values and practices to feminist ones. We haven't seen conventional organizations try to make this transition. We have, however, seen two approaches where organizations are somewhere along the path to becoming more fully feminist.

First, we've seen new businesses design feminist values into their business models from the start. Not just with the explicitly feminist bookstores, restaurants, and farms of the 1970s and beyond, or the businesses designed around the patterns of their women employees' lives (e.g., the UK's Freelance Programmers), but also more recently with entrepreneurial feminism (Orser and Elliot, 2015; FeministForums.com). We are seeing new media/digital companies (e.g., LiisBeth.com, Stocksy), consumer products businesses (e.g., LunaPads), and clothing companies (e.g., Eileen Fisher, Moxie Trades), as well as other social enterprises, aiming to put feminist values into practice throughout their business models. Although most of these enterprises are small, they are profitable and feminist. They demonstrate that it is possible to practice feminist values, make products people need, and make a profit.

A second approach is less encouraging, although businesses pursuing it have made work life better for their employees. This approach deploys ideas and practices developed by feminist businesses, advocates, and scholars, but does so without demonstrating a feminist commitment to social justice and flourishing and without crediting these feminists. Instead of demonstrating feminism, these businesses demonstrate two patriarchal power plays that I call: (1) "bropropriation," and (2) "oblivious discovery."

Bropropriation occurs when a business takes an issue or idea that feminists have advocated, strips that idea of its politics and transformational power, and then uses it to strengthen the status quo. That's how we get programs that give birth mothers, fathers, and adoptive parents identical parental leaves, while ignoring larger feminist arguments to design career paths that work for parents and non-parents, or to transform the workplace so that it supports rather than begrudgingly permits family and community life. Bropropriation is also how we get programs to "liberate" employees and build "freedom-based teams," where the definitions of freedom and liberation are so stunted that they simply mean that workers are given latitude to set their own local work goals and work times. Although it sounds revolutionary, this so-called "liberated workplace" is not where flourishing happens.

Oblivious discovery occurs when mainstream businesses "discover" ideas that feminism has been promoting and developing for quite some time. Just like when Columbus discovered Guanahari, land that was already inhabited by the Taino, cutting edge thought leaders discover new ways to engage employees, make work more meaningful, democratize decision making, and more that have already been developed in feminist theory and practice. For example, consultants recently discovered "new power", a form of power that is open, participatory, and peer-driven – and identical to the relational, connected, "jointly developing power" that Mary Parker Follett (1924) described, theorized about, and named "power-with" almost one hundred years ago. Concepts like social entrepreneurship, consensus decision-making, collective leadership, horizontal organizational structures, value networks, and co-creation are just a few of the contemporary business practices that have deep roots in feminist organizational history, theory, and practice. These newly "discovered" practices are brought into organizations as palliatives that help mitigate the problems caused by doing business as usual, but absolutely not to move the business towards social justice.

Bropropriating and colonizing feminist management ideas gives feminist initiatives partial support while ignoring the challenges they present to male privilege, masculinity, patriarchy, and dominance, as well as their commitment to justice and flourishing. Stripping the politics and the feminist legacy from these initiatives handicaps the ability of feminist ideas to transform organizations or to spark people's learning about the larger goals of feminism. Thus, we get watered down feminist practices that, while they help assuage some of the pain that gendered inequality causes so many people in so many businesses, have been made impotent against the deeper challenges of transformation.

Why aren't these change approaches more effective?

Given the complex and multi-level nature of organizational gendering practices, plus the distortions of neoliberalism and the dissimulation of postfeminism, it's no wonder that these approaches have failed to transform business. Few organizations have been able to break out of belief systems that tell us gendered inequality and feminism are unimportant, and even fewer have understood what it takes to challenge many dimensions of the gendered system simultaneously so that businesses withdraw all support for gendered dominance and the gendered structure collapses.

Some organizations are succeeding with their more circumscribed and incremental approaches, and they are closer to that interim goal where men, women, and all people work harmoniously and effectively together, happily accepting the improved, but not erased, power differences between us.

Feminism asks us to aspire for more. Feminism asks us to imagine and work towards businesses where all kinds of members have equal power to shape the culture, the systems, the interpersonal interactions, and the ways they want to show up at work, where we democratically decide on visions of the future and collectively pursue strategies for human flourishing at work, and we do work, make things, and conduct businesses that flourish.

Individual approaches for gender equality in organizations

While businesses have taken organizational-level approaches to address gender inequality, individual women have been encouraged to push for gender equality themselves. These individual strategies are often presumed to be feminist strategies because they promote the interests of at least some women. These approaches include:

1. *"Up the ladder, ladies!"*: women should strive for individual success by working harder and working more so that they can be promoted up the corporate ladder to higher and higher positions of power within a business.
2. *Be a "GirlBoss"*: women should play "hardball," and be as aggressive as men and appropriately stylish as they compete their way to the top.
3. *Deploy "feminine capital"*: women should emphasize how they bring the previously missing and now quite desirable soft skills that companies need to compete in today's world, demonstrating how they – as women – are uniquely valuable to a business.

These different approaches overlap and inform each other. They are often promoted to women as forms of feminism that are appropriate and effective in business, although, as we will see, their grasp on feminism is tenuous and provisional.

1. Up the ladder, ladies!

The approach that gets the most attention goes by many names – corporate feminism, liberal feminism, White feminism, and most recently, Lean In feminism. Lean In feminism, of course, is the approach recommended by Facebook's COO Sheryl Sandberg, in her book *Lean In: Women, Work, and the Will to Lead* (2013). I like the "up the ladder" label because it incorporates the exhortation for each woman to climb harder, because it's not just about leaning in, but also about pushing oneself higher up into positions of power.

This strategy asks women to take personal initiative and get a mentor, speak out, train themselves, take credit, step up, and exert all manner of extra effort so that their performances at work drive their rise. The recommendations of this approach are all targeted at changing the individual woman's behavior, making it play nicely with the organizational level "fix the women" strategy.

All this work happens in what is assumed to be a generally fair corporate meritocracy, where the organization will reward women commensurate with their new, improved performance. There are no other barriers for women, such as biased performance evaluations, unequal pay, or sexual harassment that leaning in or climbing harder can't overcome. And, in return for a woman's extra effort, the business can be trusted to reward her with the pay raises she negotiates for herself and give her all the maternity parking spaces she asks for.

Still, even with all this leaning in, not all women who use this strategy will succeed. Corporate ladders are designed to get narrower and have less room the closer they get to the top, ensuring that many will never rise no matter how hard they work. But regardless of whether or not an individual climber succeeds, the company she works for benefits from her additional labor.

"Up the ladder" feminism focuses on getting women to serve their companies more effectively rather than getting companies to be better places for women and men. The company has no responsibility to be proactive about helping women or all people to do better at work. If individual women don't ask for what they each need, no changes must be made. With this strategy, women can push themselves as far in and up the company as they can without upsetting the status quo.

"Up the ladder" strategies only work well for women intent on climbing the ladder, usually middle- and upper-middle-class, educationally privileged managerial women. It has little to offer the much larger group of women and people who are lower down in the employee ranks and have no career ladders to climb, not to mention those who work for a company in a contingent or contract role.

"Up the ladder" feminism assumes that individual women can solve sexism themselves, simply by working harder. And it assumes that women who climb to positions of power and authority will use this power to help other women succeed, becoming "agents of change" rather than "cogs in the machine" (Srivastava and Sherman, 2015). Agents of change might challenge stereotypes, or hire, promote, and mentor other women. These powerful women might even push the organization itself to pay women and men equally, or get family care leave for the women who clean the company's offices. Still, even as individuals move up through the hierarchy of their organization and therefore have greater potential to effect change, they may feel even greater pressure to sustain the status quo (Meyerson and Scully, 1995). Although some women in power commit to undoing gender inequality (Stainback, Kleiner, and Skaggs, 2016), women moving "up the ladder" doesn't make for much trickle down change.

Indeed, the collective promise of the "up the ladder" approach falls apart with just two words: Margaret Thatcher. Thatcher worked her way all the way up the ladder to the position of Prime Minister. Then, she used her power and position to work against the interests of the most vulnerable, including women and children. This was a decidedly anti-feminist outcome of getting a woman to the top.

2. Be a "GirlBoss"

"GirlBoss" feminism is a brash, youthful, and ultimately naive approach that tells women they'll achieve a measure of business success if they develop an aggressive attitude and update their feminine styling. I take the name "GirlBoss" feminism from the business memoir of the online fashion entrepreneur Sophia Amoroso. According to the original #GirlBoss, "You don't get taken seriously by asking someone to take you seriously. You've got to show up and own it. If this is a man's world, who cares? I'm still really glad to be a girl in it" (Amoroso, 2014, p. 17).

Can you hear the postfeminism in Amoroso's advice?

"GirlBoss" feminism advocates being loud, bold, and self-interested. It's a more fashionable, digitized, and dumbed-down version of the "Hardball for Women" advice (Heim, 1992) of the 1980s, where women in business were advised to be less accommodating and less polite in response to blatant sexism. GirlBosses should present an aggressive, rule-breaking, go-getting attitude similar to what you'd see on Shark Tank.

GirlBosses are ambitious, assertive opportunists who define success as owning your own career, charting your own path, and driving your own increasing income. They are a weird hybrid of two different gendered stereotypes. In certain elements like their appearance and their business interests (e.g., fashion and marketing over finance or manufacturing), GirlBosses are unapologetically feminine. In their behavior and attitude, they act more like privileged White men, demonstrating masculine hyper-competitiveness. Note, though, that only white women in a culture that privileges Whiteness can get away with brassy, ballsy, less feminine behaviors, because while they might challenge old-school femininity, these white women retain the racial order.

3. Deploy feminine capital

In contrast to the 'just work harder' of "climb the ladder" and the aggressive machisma of "GirlBossing," the "feminine capital" approach doubles down on pillowy soft femininity. Women are encouraged to use the unique skills and sensibilities that they have cultivated as women to create enviable success. This approach tells women to envision the feminine qualities and perspectives assigned to females as new strengths for the modern workplace. They can deploy their genderedness as a kind of work, and use it to create a place for women that is separate and different from men's place yet (purportedly) equally valuable to businesses and organizations. When women use feminine "soft skills" such as empathy, collaboration, interpersonal sensitivity, patience, community orientation, and other relational behaviors that have been gendered as feminine, they can complement and even correct the damage masculinity has caused in the workplace. And, because new forms of work increasingly depend on interpersonal skills, and management itself has become increasingly feminized (Fondas, 1997), women are poised to be even more successful at making themselves at home in the workplace.

The "feminine capital" approach is confusing, though, because it replicates the same arguments used historically for confining women to certain job roles (e.g., caregiving instead of engineering, sewing instead of welding, teaching instead of leading). What's different now is that the rationale has gone up a few pay grades so that it has infiltrated job levels (e.g., management, leadership) where women were once excluded.

Women deploying feminine capital still regularly experience their efforts as going unrecognized or even being punished. Often when women demonstrate feminine qualities, these aren't recognized as effort brought to the workplace, but instead treated as "natural" advantages of females. Natural qualities are not seen as skills worth rewarding financially (Katila and Eriksson, 2013).

Underpinning feminine capital is the conviction that women will achieve equality in business as companies come to need the qualities that women bring, whether these qualities are natural to female bodies or learned by women through conventional gendering. Thus, change relies on women bringing what businesses need, not on women being free to act or contribute as they wish, nor holding the roles they might prefer, nor simply being seen as equal to men. Not all kinds of femininities (and of course, not everything associated with being female, such as menstruation or childbearing) are considered appropriate in the workplace. One can be "too feminine" (e.g., too soft, too willing, too nice) or wrongly feminine (e.g., too maternal, too emotional). Whether deploying femininity deliberately or simply by being female in the workplace, all women and especially women of color are held to ambiguous standards of appearance and comportment, where their credibility and power depend on demonstrating "respectable business femininity" (Mavin and Grandy, 2016). Thus, this approach doesn't really make as much room for women and people as it would seem.

The first three strategies share a few blind spots:

- *There's no role for men to participate in advancing equity.* There's nothing for men to do other than to respond positively to all the climbing up, bossing around, and feminine warmth these ambitious women are contributing to the workplace. While women must work harder, be harder, and be softer, men need to do nothing. There is no effort men need to exert, nothing they need to learn, not much they need to change.

- *These approaches don't ask women who do advance to take responsibility for helping others.* They don't address how these successful women should use their increasing power and authority to advocate for changes that will benefit all women as well as men. There are no strategies for building solidarity and community among women and no strategies for building alliances with men to improve the workplace for everyone.

- *They have no organizational change mandate.* Women and people who want to achieve parity for themselves also have a role to play in improving the organization itself. When women who focus on their own advancement ask companies only to assimilate them, not to transform, the companies miss growth opportunities that pressure to change might have triggered. And they miss the inspiration of envisioning a flourishing future.

- *These approaches don't help and often hurt the women who pursue them.* When women and people hear messages about individual female empowerment, such as "lean in," "GirlBoss," and "feminine capital," they place more responsibility, and consequently more blame, on themselves and on other individual women for the inequalities they experience. Feminine capital approaches can also limit what women feel they are capable of. Simply labeling certain behaviors as masculine and feminine takes them out of the psychic toolkit of many women, making it harder for them to perform these behaviors in the workplace (Martin and Phillips, 2018). Yet, when these same leaderly, takecharge behaviors are described as "agency" – a gender-neutral term – women's workplace confidence and action taking is increased. Further, leaning in, being bold, or being feminine often trigger conflicting, negative, and counterproductive responses from coworkers and the organization itself (Carli and Eagly, 2007; Crobot-Mason, Hoobler, and Burno, 2018).

- *The individual emphasis of these approaches diminishes people's awareness of systemic obstacles and their interest in addressing them.* In other words, these messages mute the analysis and suppress the action needed to address the rest of the gender structure (Kim, Fitzsimons, and Kay, 2018). This is a problem because the obstacles to gender equality are beyond any individual's control, and require collective action directed at the system.

These approaches depend on a hyper-individualistic, autonomous, self-centered female self to single-handedly improve the world as a potential but not guaranteed side effect of her own success. In truth, individual women are minor players in this game of gender inequality. They can't change the rules in the magic circle. To eliminate gendered inequality, women, people, and businesses must collectively address the systems that recreate and reinforce inequality.

4. Feminist advocacy and issue-based activism

There is at least one additional approach available for individual women, men, and people who want to advocate on behalf of gender equality and feminist ideas within a business. This approach addresses not the individual employee's own success, but rather collective change for all women and people in their workplace. This strategy is feminist advocacy and includes several forms of resistance (Thomas and Davies, 2005), tempered radicalism, and issue-based activism.

Feminist advocacy (Harquail, 1996) includes actions that range from speaking up about gender equality initiatives, to using one's organizational role to support individual women, feminists, and change agents, to teaching others about feminism, and more. Advocacy can be protective of women's interests or serve as resistance to specific sexist norms and events (e.g., challenging an all-male speaker panel). Advocacy can also be more proactive, such as creating a speakers' website that features diverse voices, or suggesting that a feminist value help shape a product's design.

Feminist advocacy differs dramatically from the previous three individual strategies because it is intended not to promote one's own career prospects, but rather to change the organization's gendered structure to help it advance towards gender equality. Feminist advocates in the workplace are often "tempered radicals" (Meyerson and Scully, 1995), individuals who are committed both to their organization's success and to a cause that challenges the dominant culture of their organization. Feminist advocacy can feel risky if advocates believe they'll damage their career prospects (Ashford et al., 1998). Advocacy can be dangerous for people of color and white women, who are penalized in performance ratings when they advocate for gender and diversity initiatives (Hekman et al., 2017).

Advocates' concerns about how their efforts will be received can lead them to make subtle, small-scale, local changes, especially when they lack organizational power and resources to implement wider changes. Thus, everyday feminist advocacy often focuses on influencing colleagues to think or act differently. Small changes by insiders can contribute to awareness and help set the stage for larger actions. Well-placed individuals can use their organizationally sanctioned positions of power, authority, and influence to make decisions that advance gender equality. For example, advocates with organizational power can set and execute their own inclusion mandates, just as filmmaker Ava DuVernay does when she deliberately hires mostly people of color and white women as directors, camera operators, and producers.

Advocates can also network and band together with other advocates inside their organizations and across their industries using issue-based activism. Employee activists leverage a larger cultural conversation, as well as examples set in other businesses, to strengthen their hand as they propose gender equality initiatives to their companies.

In the past few years, we have seen feminist issues – like marriage equality, Black Lives Matter, wage equity, women's representation on industry panels, and sexual harassment to name a few – move from the popular conversation into business-specific initiatives, led by feminists and other activists within individual companies. These grassroots efforts are sometimes loosely, and other times closely, coupled to political or social activist groups outside a company. Employee activists use the cultural attention drawn to the issue to add additional legitimacy to their internal gender equity initiative and add urgency to their demands for action by their business. It doesn't hurt that companies can publicly demonstrate some commitment to addressing the culturally hot issue by finally responding to their own employees' proposals.

Consider, for example, the 2018 initiative of women at Nike's headquarters. A small group covertly surveyed other female employees about their experiences with sexual harassment, gender discrimination, gender imbalance among company leaders, and ongoing pay disparities (Creswell, Draper, and Abrams, 2018). The group delivered their survey data to Nike's CEO along with a request for company-wide change. The CEO responded to both the hard numbers and the attention brought by the #MeToo conversation and dismissed several male executives. Nike then reviewed and changed its human resources operations in ways designed to reduce not only sexual harassment but ultimately also other gendered unequal policies (Zetlin, 2018). This organizational-level change, on a few key and timely issues, was led by a cadre of feminist employees.

Similarly, at the *New York Times* (Goldstein, 2017) and at Amazon's headquarters (Gale, 2017), small groups of women managers met to research, gather data, and develop proposals for expanded child leave policies. Each group presented their proposals to top management, who ultimately implemented most of the policy recommendations. At Google, employees banded together to advocate against building products to comply with China's censorship policies, citing ethical and justice-related concerns. All this advocacy may sound straightforward, so it's important to remember that this work is arduous, time-intensive, and politically sensitive, done by advocates on top of and in addition to their regular paid jobs.

Gateway feminism: entry points to the revolution

Given just these initial criticisms of both organization-level and individual-level approaches to gender equality in business, can you imagine any of them getting us closer to the flourishing work and life that feminism seeks to achieve? These approaches draw on feminist language, feminist imagery, and feminist energy, but not all of them are feminist approaches themselves. Fully feminist approaches would:

1. Focus on deep structural change to challenge the gender structure and inequality regimes and to reshape culture,
2. Focus on collective action to help each other and women as a group, not just individual actions to help oneself or one's own organization,

3. Invite and expect men and all people to participate in developing and unfolding paths to equality and flourishing,
4. Demonstrate all five feminist values, and
5. Fully commit to a vision of a just future where everyone flourishes.

If some approaches aimed at helping women succeed aren't feminism, what are they? It helps to think of them as forms of what feminist writer Roxanne Gay (2014) calls "gateway feminism." Considering what kind of feminist role model Beyoncé offers, Gay explains "[Beyoncé] is *one* woman – an amazing woman to be sure – but she is a gateway to feminism, not the movement itself" (emphasis in original). Like Beyoncé, most of these approaches are ways to get into feminism (or get feminism into business), but they aren't feminism itself. Gateway feminism isn't the movement, it's an entry point. It can be a great entry point, or a disappointing one, but it is a start.

As if equality and flourishing for all people needs to be made more appealing somehow, gateway feminisms aim to make it look easier for individual women and/or organizations to move closer towards gender equality by simplifying, hiding, or just plain dropping the political messages of feminism. This means these approaches are not only less pointed, less acute, and less powerful, but also less demanding of real change, because they rarely, if ever, challenge the status quo.

But, feminism properly understood must threaten the status quo by challenging the gendered inequalities and the acceptance of dominance that systems of inequalities support. The reason that any of these individual level or organizational level approaches have been adopted at all is that they are the strategies that can be fitted most easily into the value systems that modern companies, modern managers, and contemporary capitalism depend on. These approaches are merely gateways and not expressways to getting feminism into business.

We now know a great deal about how to add women and stir, fix the women, value femininity, and fine tune policies in organizations. We don't, however, hear quite as much about how to make deep cultural change, how to fix gender structure at all levels, or how to transform the total system. And, while there are any number of popular business books marketed to women who want to lean in, become GirlBosses, or deploy their female advantage, there are virtually no books telling women and feminists within business how to band together, develop policies, and push for organizational change towards justice and flourishing. Gateway feminism is popular; it doesn't work as well but it sure sells better than the real thing.

Some argue that these gateway approaches to equality do more harm than good. They take lots of hard work by the people and companies attempting them, and they divert attention away from other approaches that might be more transformational. These concerns are real. But I'm disinclined to dismiss these efforts or roll my eyes at these approaches and their champions, because for all their potential issues and limitations, these approaches can help people and companies begin to learn how to practice feminism. And, while they are learning, women (and men, and companies) are alleviating some inequalities and helping to enable a few more people to contribute and participate as full human beings.

Ultimately, however, whether these are organizationally or individually driven initiatives there is an insurmountable bias working against all of them: the needs of the business always seem to take priority over the needs of equality. Women can be promoted, accommodated, and trained, and even be influential in redesigning some part of a business, as long as the overall profit motive and power structure of the business remain in place. Thus, most change initiatives are suspect because they are conceived, designed, marketed, responded to, or executed only if, when, and how they add to a business's profits, no matter how much they fail or help to bring about gender equality. What's even more regrettable is that few businesses aim higher: to recreate themselves as profitable, effective companies where everyone flourishes.

QUESTIONS

1. Where else have you heard neoliberalism influence people's expectations of business?
2. What do you believe about business's role in achieving gender equality? What caveats, boundary conditions, or concerns are raised for you?
3. Which of these organizational and individual approaches have you seen in action? How well have they seemed to work?
4. How do these individual level and organizational level strategies fit together? What combinations are sympathetic matches, and what combinations set up a clash of perspectives and visions? How might these clashes be reconciled?

REFERENCES

Acker, J., 1990. 'Hierarchies, Jobs, Bodies: A Theory of Gendered Organizations'. *Gender and Society*, 4(2), pp. 139–158.

Acker, J., 2006. 'Inequality Regimes: Gender, Class, and Race in Organizations'. *Gender and Society*, 20(4), p. 441–464.

Alvesson, M. and Billing, Y.D., 2002. 'Beyond Body-Counting: A Discussion of the Social Construction of Gender at Work'. In: I. Aaltio and A.J. Mills, eds, *Gender, Identity, and the Culture of Organizations*, London, Routledge, pp. 72–91.

Amoruso, S., 2014. *#GIRLBOSS*, New York, Penguin.

Ashford, S.J., Rothbard, N.P., Piderit, S.K., and Dutton, J.E., 1998. 'Out on a Limb: The Role of Context and Impression Management in Selling Gender-Equity Issues'. *Administrative Science Quarterly*, 43(1), pp. 23–57.

Becker, J.C. and Swim, J.K., 2011. 'Seeing the Unseen: Attention to Daily Encounters with Sexism as Way to Reduce Sexist Beliefs'. *Psychology of Women Quarterly*, 35(2), pp. 227–242.

Bohnet, I., 2016. *What Works: Gender Equality by Design*, Cambridge, MA, Belknap Press.

Calás, M.B. and Smircich, L., 1996. 'From the "Women's Point of View": Feminist approaches to Organization Studies'. In: S.R. Clegg, C. Hardy, and W.R. Nord, eds, *Handbook of Organization Studies*, London, Sage, pp. 218–257.

Calder-Dawe, O., 2015. 'The Choreography of Everyday Sexism: Reworking Sexism in Interaction'. *New Formations*, 86, pp. 89–105.

Carli, L.L. and Eagly, A.H., 2007. *Through the Labyrinth: The Truth about How Women Become Leaders*, Cambridge, MA, Harvard Business School Press.

Correll, S.J., 2017. 'SWS 2016 Feminist Lecture: Reducing Gender Biases in Modern Workplaces: A Small Wins Approach to Organizational Change'. *Gender and Society*, 31(6), pp. 725–750.

Creswell, J., Draper, K., and Abrams, R., 2018. 'At Nike, Revolt Led by Women Leads to Exodus of Male Executives', *The New York Times*. Available at: www.nytimes.com/2018/04/28/business/nike-women.html. Accessed: October 1 2018.

Crobot-Mason, D., Hoobler, J.M., and Burno, J., 2018. 'Lean in Versus the Literature: An Evidence-Based Examination'. *Academy of Management Perspectives*, 33(1), pp. 110–130.

Crosby, F., 1984. 'The Denial of Personal Discrimination'. *American Behavioral Scientist*, 27(3), pp. 371–386.

Ely, R.J. and Meyerson, D.E., 2000. 'Advancing Gender Equity in Organizations: The Challenge and Importance of Maintaining a Gender Narrative'. *Organization*, 7(4), pp. 589–608.

Follett, M.P., 1924. *Creative Experience*, New York, Longmans.

Fondas, N., 1997. 'Feminization Unveiled: Management Qualities in Contemporary Writings'. *Academy of Management Review*, 22(1), pp. 257–282.

Gale, R., 2017. 'How the Women of Amazon Fought for–and Won–a Revolutionary Family Leave Policy', *Slate*. Available at: www.slate.com/blogs/better_life_lab/2017/10/10/amazon_s_paid_leave_it_all_started_with_wine_and_chocolate_in_one_mom_s.html. Accessed: October 15 2018.

Gay, R., 2014. 'Emma Watson? Jennifer Lawrence? These Aren't the Feminists You're Looking For'. *The Guardian*. Available at: www.theguardian.com/commentisfree/2014/oct/10/-sp-jennifer-lawrence-emma-watson-feminists-celebrity. Accessed: October 14 2016.

Giddens, A., 1984. *The Constitution of Society*, Cambridge, UK, Polity Press.

Gill, R., 2008. 'Culture and Subjectivity in Neoliberal and Postfeminist Times'. *Subjectivity*, 25(1), pp. 432–445.

Gill, R., 2014. 'Unspeakable Inequalities: Post Feminism, Entrepreneurial Subjectivity, and the Repudiation of Sexism among Cultural Workers'. *Social Politics: International Studies in Gender, State and Society*, 21(4), pp. 509–528.

Gill, R. and Orgad, S., 2017. 'Confidence Culture and the Remaking of Feminism'. *New Formations*, 91, pp. 16–34.

Gill, R., Kelan, E.K., and Scharff, C.M., 2017. 'A Postfeminist Sensibility at Work'. *Gender, Work and Organization*, 24(3), pp. 226–244.

Goldstein, K., 2017. 'Where Are the Mothers?', *Nieman Reports*. Available at: http://niemanreports.org/articles/where-are-the-mothers/. Accessed: July 26 2017.

Halford, S. and Leonard, P., 2001. *Gender, Power and Organizations*, New York, Palgrave.

Harquail, C.V., 1996. 'When One Speaks for Many: The Influence of Social Identification on Group Advocacy in Organizations'. Ph.D. dissertation, University of Michigan, Ann Arbor, MI.

Heim, P., 1992. *Hardball for Women: Winning at the Game of Business*. Los Angeles, CA, Lowell House.

Hekman, D.R., Johnson, S.K., Foo, M.W., and Yang, W., 2017. 'Does Diversity-Valuing Behavior Result in Diminished Performance Ratings for Non-White and Female Leaders?'. *Academy of Management Journal*, 60(2), pp. 771–797.

Helgesen, S., 1995. *The Female Advantage: Women's Ways of Leadership*. New York, Doubleday.

Hills, R., 2014. 'Laurie Penny's In-Your-Face Feminism'. *The Daily Beast*. Available at: www.thedailybeast.com/laurie-pennys-in-your-face-feminism. Accessed: February 12 2018.

Hirst, A. and Schwabenland, C., 2018. 'Doing Gender in the "New Office"'. *Gender, Work and Organization*, 25(2), pp. 159–176.

Katila, S. and Eriksson, P., 2013. 'He Is a Firm, Strong-Minded and Empowering Leader, but Is She? Gendered Positioning of Female and Male CEOs'. *Gender, Work and Organization*, 20(1), pp. 71–84.

Kelan, E.K., 2009. 'Gender Fatigue: The Ideological Dilemma of Gender Neutrality and Discrimination in Organizations'. *Canadian Journal of Administrative Sciences/Revue Canadienne des Sciences de l'Administration*, 26(3), pp. 197–210.

Kim, J.Y., Fitzsimons, G. and Kay, A., 2018. 'Conflating a Solution with a Cause: The Potential Harmful Effects of Women's Empowerment Messages'. *Academy of Management Proceedings*, 2018(1), p. 12537.

Kolb, D., Fletcher, J., Meyerson, D., Merrill-Sands, D., and Ely, R., 1998. 'Making Change: A Framework for Promoting Gender Equity in Organizations'. *Center for Gender and Organizations Insights*, 3(2), pp. 2–4.

McRobbie, A., 2009. *The Aftermath of Feminism: Gender, Culture and Social Change*, London, Sage.

Martin, A.E. and Phillips, K.W., 2018. 'Power of a Label: When Masculinity Is Replaced with Agency Women Feel More Confident and Take Action'. *Academy of Management Proceedings*, 2018(1), p. 15534.

Mavin, S. and Grandy, G., 2016. 'Women Elite Leaders Doing Respectable Business Femininity: How Privilege Is Conferred, Contested and Defended through the Body'. *Gender, Work and Organization*, 23(4), pp. 379–396.

Meyerson, D.E. and Scully, M.A., 1995. 'Crossroads Tempered Radicalism and the Politics of Ambivalence and Change'. *Organization Science*, 6(5), pp. 585–600.

Monteverde, G., 2014. 'Not All Feminist Ideas Are Equal: Anti-Capitalist Feminism and Female Complicity'. *Journal of International Women's Studies*, 16(1), pp. 62–75.

Orser, B. and Elliott, C., 2015. *Feminine Capital: Unlocking the Power of Women Entrepreneurs*. Redwood City, CA, Stanford Business Books.

Ortlieb, R. and Sieben, B., 2017. 'Balls, Barbecues and Boxing: Contesting Gender Regimes at Organizational Social Events'. *Organization Studies*, 40, pp. 1–19.

Radoynovska, N.M. 2018. Working within discretionary boundaries: Allocative rules, exceptions, and the microfoundations of inequality. *Organization Studies*, 39, pp. 1277–1298.

Rafaeli, A., Dutton, J.E., Harquail, C.V., and Mackie-Lewis, S., 1997. 'Navigating by Attire: The Use of Dress by Female Administrative Employees'. *Academy of Management Journal*, 4(1), pp. 8–45.

Reuters, May 21 2013, "Pope criticizes 'savage capitalism' on visit to food kitchen", www.reuters.com/article/us-pope-capitalism/pope-criticizes-savage-capitalism-on-visit-to-food-kitchen-idUSBRE94K12K20130521. Accessed: April 11 2019.

Riley, S., 2001. 'Maintaining Power: Male Constructions of "Feminists" and "Feminist" Values'. *Feminism and Psychology*, 11(1), pp. 55–78.

Rosener, J.B., 1990. 'Ways Women Lead'. *Harvard Business Review*, 68(6), pp. 119–125.

Sandberg, S., 2013. *Lean in: Women, Work, and the Will to Lead*, New York, Knopf.

Smith, C. and Turner, S., 2005. 'The Radical Transformation of Diversity and Inclusion: The Millennial Influence'. Available at: www2.deloitte.com/content/dam/Deloitte/us/Documents/about-deloitte/us-inclus-millennial-influence-120215.pdf. Accessed: October 10 2018.

Srivastava, S.B. and Sherman, E.L., 2015. 'Agents of Change or Cogs in the Machine? Reexamining the Influence of Female Managers on the Gender Wage Gap'. *American Journal of Sociology*, 120(6), pp. 1778–1808.

Stafford, M. 2013. 'Can Savage Capitalism Be Humanized? Taking up the Challenge of Pope Francis'. *ABC News*. Available at: www.abc.net.au/religion/articles/2013/08/20/3829726.htm. Accessed: October 10 2018.

Stainback, K., Kleiner, S., and Skaggs, S., 2016. 'Women in Power: Undoing or Redoing the Gendered Organization?'. *Gender and Society*, 30(1), pp. 109–135.

Thomas, R. and Davies, A., 2005. 'What Have the Feminists Done for Us? Feminist Theory and Organizational Resistance'. *Organization*, 12(5), pp. 711–740.

Zetlin, M., 2018. 'Women at Nike Fight Hostile Culture with a Simple but Effective Tool That You Can Use Too', *Inc. Magazine*. Available at: www.inc.com/minda-zetlin/nike-sexual-harassment-survey-gender-bias-executives-fired-trevor-edwards.html. Accessed: 15 October 2018.

3

FEMINIST INTERVENTIONS IN CORE BUSINESS CONCEPTS

INTRODUCTION

Chapter 3 brings feminist values to bear on the content of specific management conversations to help us understand how feminism has challenged conventional business thinking. First, we contrast the conventional and feminist answers to three big picture questions about business. This contrast allows us to identify themes that will appear throughout the sections on specific topics that follow, as well as in feminist conversations about most other business concepts. Organized by this overview, we will consider how asking questions related to feminist values have changed the conversation about eight core management topics.

COMPARING CONVENTIONAL AND FEMINIST PERSPECTIVES

Conventional business and feminist business perspectives have very different approaches to three central questions:

1. What should be the goals of business and work?
2. How should collective control and coordination be achieved?
3. What values will lead to a business's success?

To help you anticipate, organize, and focus the feminist critique of business, Table 3.1 outlines some key ways that conventional business and feminism answer these important questions.

Conventional businesses emphasize concepts in the left column, and feminist perspectives emphasize concepts in the right column. Both columns are strategic simplifications of these perspectives. Although the table is set up in two columns,

Table 3.1 Contrasting conventional and feminist views of business

Conventional Practice	Feminist View
Q1. What should be the goals of business and work?	
Production	Reproduction
Extraction	Regeneration
Profit for owners	Financial and other value for everyone
Transactions	Relationships
Organizational needs	Individual and community needs
Wealth accumulation	Provisioning and resourcing to support quality of life
Market orientation	Community orientation
Q2. How should collective control and coordination be achieved?	
Dominance, achieved through power-over	Mutuality, achieved through power-with
Hierarchical structure and relationships, assumptions of superiority	Flat, peer-to-peer networks, assumptions of equivalence
Competition	Cooperation and collaboration
Scarcity thinking	Abundance thinking
Ownership of few over many	Shared ownership
Q3. What values will lead to business success?	
Individual achievement, self-actualization	Flourishing for everyone
Autonomy	Interindependence
Instrumental orientation: valued for utility	Intrinsic value: valued for its own sake
Meritocratic ideology	Equality and equity
Androcentric: male as model, others as "others"	Inclusive: "universal design" that recognizes important differences and fits everyone
Hegemonic masculinity	Gender multiplicity and equality

this is not to put the concepts in a binary, either/or relationship. Either/or thinking causes people to favor one view over another, ending up with dominant and marginalized perspectives. Feminism argues for 'both/and' thinking that considers that both options might have value and that there might be additional options to consider too.

Q1. What should be the goals of business and work?

Conventionally, we understand that the goal of a business is to make and sell things to generate profits. Profits will reward the owners and investors for their investment of money, and wages will reward the employees for their investment of time and energy. Employees' wages form their livelihood and help support their dependents. Businesses generate profits so that owners can accumulate wealth. Businesses prioritize the needs of the owners and the organization over those of employees as a group, focus on producing things that can be sold, and emphasize transactional exchanges (e.g., time for money, money for product, ownership stake for capital investment) within a marketplace. Businesses emphasize the efficient use of resources, which means they aim to extract the most that they can from the resources they use while paying as little as possible for their use of them.

The feminist view, in contrast, defines the goal of a business as providing what people and communities need to live good lives through the products the business creates, the wages the business pays, and the work that the business engages in. Feminist business focuses not on wealth accumulation for a few but on "provisioning" (Ferber and Nelson, 1993; Power, 2004), the goal of providing everyone with basic goods and services, and creating and distributing things necessary for life. They seek abundance for everyone rather than wealth for the few. A feminist view of business also takes a full cycle, full systems perspective to address both production and reproduction. It cares not only about extracting value from resources but also about regenerating, renewing, and recycling these resources. The full cycle, full systems view of feminist business refuses to separate transactions from relationships, and instead recognizes that the goal of a business is to create mutually sustaining relationships among all stakeholders.

Q2. How should collective coordination and control be achieved?

Organizations bring people and interests together and coordinate and control all the disparate actors, interests, and activities needed to achieve the business's goals. In conventional business thinking, the mechanisms for coordinating different interests and offering shared direction emphasize dominance and obedience, power and submission. Control and coordination can be achieved through the formal structure of an organization by reporting relationships, formal authority, methods for disciplining and punishing, and motivating and rewarding stakeholders. With detachment, neutrality, and rationality, processes should be broken down into components to produce the most efficient outcomes (Mumby and Putman, 1992).

Conventional businesses assume that dominance (and the force that it implies) is something to strive for. Just think about the concept of market domination. Whether it's customer mindshare or a subordinate's responsiveness, having power over others seems appropriate in conventional business.

In contrast to conventional business's reliance on domination to generate power and authority, feminist business thinking emphasizes developing "power-with" (Follett, 1924) other people, groups, and actors, through mutual recognition and for mutual gain. Feminist business emphasizes power that comes from consent and by building relationships (aka power-with), as well as individuals' power-to that reflects agency. Rather than relying on competition, fighting and "winner takes all" logic, feminist business thinking demotes competition to a more limited role. Instead, it prioritizes cooperation, collaboration, and mutual benefit. Rather than demonstrating a "bias towards capital (Kelly, 2003) and restricting ownership of the firm, the firm's outcomes, and the firms' profits to the few who provide financial resources, ownership and profit also accrue to those who provide labor, energy, creativity, and time. Feminist business thinking finds organizational authority not in those who supply the company's capital, but in the democratic consensus of central stakeholders, all of whom participate in key decision-making.

Coordination and control in conventional businesses depend on hierarchies where those higher up have authority and status over those below them. The higher a person is, the more important they are relative to those below them. Feminists, with their emphasis on equality among individuals, prefer organizational structures that reflect peer-to-peer relationships, networks, and webs (Helgesen, 1995; McKinney, 2015). Still, feminists believe that some hierarchy where differences in authority are based on legitimate authority (e.g., expertise, democratic representation, constitutional structure) is appropriate and functional (Freeman, 1972).

Q3. What values will lead to business success?

Each perspective emphasizes the values that shape their worldview. Believing that autonomy and sovereign independence is the most desired state of human accomplishment, conventional business emphasizes individual achievement and self-actualization. People and actions are valued to the degree that they help the individual and the organization achieve their goals. Believing that organizations are rational and designed as gender- and race-blind meritocracies suggests that anyone can succeed and that the cream will naturally rise to the top (Seron et al., 2018).

Men/male/masculine employees are the norm and the ideal. Thus, anything that fits with the androcentric, male model is good. Anything that doesn't fit the male default is not only abnormal, but also tainted. For example, masculine rationality is associated with good business practice, while feminine emotionality is bad for business (Dougherty and Drumheller, 2006). Therefore, individual behavior and organizational systems should reinforce a hierarchy that privileges men, male-typed behaviors, and masculine characteristics because these will lead to individual and organizational success. Meanwhile, demonstrating female-typed behaviors and feminine characteristics is not only less valued and less valuable, but may also contribute to failure.

Within the feminist business worldview, the goal of business is not simply individual achievement or organizational success, but also includes flourishing for everyone. Interindependence, knowing that each must contribute their own strength to support the group's success and that the group must be strong to provide support for the individual's success, replaces conventional business's focus on detached, stand-alone independence. People, actions, and outcomes are valued not simply for what they help us achieve but also for their own sake, for the world being a better place because they exist. This means, for example, that all employees are valued as human beings, regardless of how efficient they are as workers. Neither their work performance nor their jobs' status determines their social value. Organizations, roles, and work should be designed so that they can use the skills and fit the bodies of any human, not just male ones, with a kind of universal design that recognizes important differences and fits the vast majority. Universal design makes it possible for people to contribute and succeed when they behave in ways that are not male-typed or masculine but instead reflect their own understanding of their gender genre and style.

For all three questions, conventional perspectives and feminist perspectives differ significantly. Feminist views emphasize values, processes, and goals that are simply not part of the conventional business perspective.

Box 3.1 EARLY FEMINIST MANAGEMENT THINKERS

There are many early management scholars, activists, and business people who worked to bring women's interests and experiences to the fore, and who also aimed to demonstrate feminist values in how they theorized about and/or managed businesses (Paludi, HelmsMills, and Mills, 2014). Although the complete history of women's and feminists' management thinking has yet to be written, these five women are broadly recognized as having advanced feminist ideas in management.

Mary Parker Follett (1868–1933)

Mary Parker Follett was a political philosopher, management theorist, advisor to business, and social worker who drew on her early experiences organizing communities of workers to develop her ideas about coordination, leadership, and management (Graham, 1995). Follett offered original formulations of a broad range of topics common in management, especially ones relevant to feminist approaches. These topics include:

- "Power-with" as an alternative to top-down "power-over."
- Empowerment (now sometimes called power-within): the idea that each person has to grow their own power.
- "Relationality": an emphasis on the connections between individuals and among groups, and between individuals, groups, and the environment. Seen as a foundation for care-centered management and systems thinking (O'Mahony, 2018).
- Reciprocal relationships, horizontal organizing, peer-to-peer influence, and networked coordination.
- Transformational leadership.
- "The law of the situation": emphasizing letting the work lead what needs to be done, rather than letting players dictate their preferences.

- "Win–win" conflict resolution: rejecting compromise as a way of dealing with difference and believing that differences must be worked out in everyday action together.
- Integrative conflict resolution: problem-solving via dialogue and action in local and diverse networks and organizations as the basis for both good management and democracy.
- Circular response: recognizing that behavior helps to create the situation to which people respond, in a feedback loop of self-reinforcing interpretations and actions.

Many of Follett's ideas came back into vogue in the 1970's human relations movement, under labels like job enrichment, employee involvement, job redesign, workplace democracy, and quality of work life (Nohria, 1995). Few scholars mentioned Follett's articulations of these ideas, and some took her concepts and examples without even citing her written work.

Follett was deeply interested in how individuals could have productive lives by optimizing themselves within groups and relationships. She rejected mechanistic understandings of human behavior, and understood behavior to be a function of the relationship between individuals and between individuals and the environment. Follett criticized hierarchical organizations, competition, and the "command and control" patriarchal leadership style. She highlighted the role of social justice as a collective and progressive achievement developed through community and produced through day-to-day interactions.

Francis Perkins (1880–1965)

Francis Perkins was a social worker, lobbyist, and policymaker best known for her contributions as U.S. Secretary of Labor from 1933 to 1945. Perkins was one of the first national policymakers to focus on the concerns of wage workers. She challenged conventional management practice through her design of the Social Security Act of 1934, which established not only pensions for aging workers, but also workers' compensation, unemployment insurance, maternal and child health services, and direct aid to the poor and the disabled. She also promoted the Fair Labor Standards Act of 1938, which outlawed most child labor and established a federal minimum wage, a system of overtime pay, an eight-hour workday, and, for most workers, a 40-hour work week (Downey, 2009).

Driven by concern for workers' health and security both in and outside the workplace, Perkins' insisted that managers pay more attention to the needs of employees. This concern for workers' whole lives was one of the first expressions of the feminist ethic of care (Prieto et al., 2016) in management conversation. For Perkins, labor was not a commodity, but a socially and individually valuable and productive expression of human life and personality. Because she believed that business could be simultaneously humane and profitable, Perkins argued that demonstrating concern for workers defined a "good" business. Although several of Perkins' contributions were later adopted by and credited to male management scholars, Perkins is recognized as having developed revolutionary ways to conceive of organizing, managing, and business (Williams and Mills, 2017).

Mary Van Kleeck (1883–1972)

American activist, researcher, and labor organizer Mary Van Kleeck worked to protect and advance worker's lives, to expand scientific management, and to encourage the adoption of a planned economy (Selmi and Hunter, 2001). Her research and advocacy related to "women in industry" led her to diagnose poor working conditions and unemployment as the fault of inefficient management. Van Kleeck believed that scientific management (aka Taylorism) could resolve worker dissatisfaction (especially with repetitive and meaningless work), injuries, and poor living standards while at the same time benefiting business. Moreover, scientific, professional management could "make industry and all its results in human lives harmonize with our ideals for the community" (Van Kleeck, 1924, in Alchon, 1991, 19).

Van Kleeck was also an early technocrat, believing that technology rightly used could resolve worker, business, and economic issues revealed by the Great Depression. As the Director of Industrial Studies for the Russell Sage Foundation, Van Kleeck's radical proposals for social-economic planning drew on insights from early Soviet communism. Her connection to socialist ideas, her concern for wage laborers' working conditions, her interest in their health and family lives, and her belief that businesses would improve when labor asserted its power, all help to explain why Van Kleeck's work has been overlooked (Alchon, 1991).

Dame Stephanie Shirley (1933–)

Using a man's name to get the attention of potential clients, Stephanie (Steve) Shirley founded the software development firm Freelance Programmers (FI) in 1959 so that she and other women with computing skills and children could stay employed part-time or on a project basis. FI's ad hoc teams of programmers worked remotely from their homes, with phone calls banned at mealtime and after 9 pm to keep them free for family responsibilities. Shirley explains, "I had merely imagined a workplace undisfigured by traditional male sexism" (Shirley, 2012, p. 79).

To Shirley, a pro-woman, pro-caregiver policy was a business opportunity. FI was "a company that would offer opportunities to the kind of woman whom traditional male-dominated companies considered unemployable" (Shirley, 2012, p. 78). Among these women engineers, FI developed a female-oriented, family-oriented work structure and a feminist culture. FI's workforce expanded beyond women with children to include any engineer with any kind of dependents, but its mission never changed. Before Shirley took the firm public in 1996, she engineered an employee buyout that allowed her to extend ownership to early employees, over 70 of whom became millionaires because of these stock grants.

Dame Anita Roddick (1942–2007)

Anita Roddick, founder of The Body Shop, an international retail chain selling natural beauty products, was one of the best-known entrepreneurial feminists. She centered her organization around feminist principles of love, care, and intuition (Roddick, 1991, p. 17). An outspoken, self-identified feminist, Roddick was also an advocate for human rights, animal rights, and environmentalism. In the marketplace, she encouraged a feminist orientation towards internal rather than external beauty and directed the company's product positioning to celebrate the customer as she is, rather than as a fantasy. Roddick stressed the wisdom that comes from lived experience, explaining that as a female consumer herself, she understood what women customers might want.

Organizationally, The Body Shop under Roddick's direction had a high proportion of female executives and middle managers, as well as retail employees. She prioritized the company's mission and principles, advocating for diversity, fair trade, and green consumerism (Martin, Knopoff, and Beckman, 1998). She used her business as a tool for social change and the stores for connecting customers with the company's advocacy. Roddick was one of the first entrepreneurs and feminists to demonstrate at a global scale that purpose could drive profits and that ethical supply chain practices could contribute to justice.

FEMINIST INTERVENTIONS IN CORE BUSINESS CONCEPTS

Organized by this big picture contrast, we turn to a selection of management, business, and organization topics. By intervening in how we think about these topics, feminists have been changing the assumptions of these conversations, expanding their purview, and transforming how managers, students, business people, and employees understand these core constructs and how they should be addressed in business.

Which topics should we focus on when applying feminism to business?

Feminism's intervention into business thinking is so comprehensive that there is a feminist take on every issue and every topic in management, from authority to zero-sum transactions. Every business topic could benefit from feminist intervention, but only a representative few can be discussed in this small space.

To select the eight topics following, I focused on the concepts that most business people might expect feminism to address in business. The topics include chronic challenges in management practice as well as more familiar issues that are regularly labeled as "gender issues" in the business and popular press. If the topics or questions feel unfamiliar at first, reflect on your own organizational experiences to ground them as you read.

Some of these sections consider related themes, such as questions about work and the organization of work, but each section addresses these questions from different directions and with different concerns. Because the sections have been written to stand alone, some themes will appear in more than one conversation.

The sections offer a feminist take on:

1. Redefining "work" and re-centering the economy.
2. Work–family–life conflict.
3. Gendered work, gendered wages.
4. Foundations of organizational structure.
5. Reconsidering organizational culture.
6. Bodies in the workplace.
7. Harmful workplace experiences.
8. Models of leadership and expressions of power.

Of course, there are topics readers might hope to see that aren't included on this list, such as capitalism, sexual orientation, masculinity, entrepreneurship, diversity and inclusion, and many more (find additional feminist analyses of business topics on my website, cvharquail.com). Even with these eight topics, we have space only for an introduction and not a complete investigation. For the topics addressed following, as well as topics you hope to address yourself, let this section demonstrate and invite new ways to question the way things are, as well as new ways to appreciate how they could be different, and better, for everyone.

Redefining "work" and re-centering the economy

Few concepts are as fundamental to a business as the notion of work. Work is the reason we gather together in a business. Work is what we pay employees to do, how we evaluate employees' performance, what we're always seeking to improve, and what we aim to coordinate and control. And, of course, work produces what customers need and leads to returns on investment for business owners. "Work" is any person's activity that generates economic, social, community, and political value.

Economists and others have defined "work" in ways that serve the interests of the business and its owners. Feminists' efforts to consider everyone's interests and experiences in what we count as "work" (Cameron and Gibson-Graham, 2003) have critiqued, expanded, and refashioned our understanding of work, by:

- Making more kinds of work visible and equally valuable,
- Challenging the idea that types of work can be conceptualized as separate when they are inextricably connected,
- Challenging the ways that some effortful activity in the workplace counts as "work" while other essential activity does not,
- Questioning why who does the work influences whether that work is recognized, and
- Questioning how we value work versus other life activities.

Feminists have sought to recognize all manner of human effort and intention that goes into being an effective employee. This advocacy aims to give credit and value to the work and the workers that contribute to business, to society, and to human flourishing.

Why redefining work matters

Feminists have noted that, when it's all said and done, the various schemes for categorizing and differentiating types of work either serve or resist the same purpose: to help us put one kind of work, one place of work, one outcome of work, one beneficiary of work ahead of others. This differentiating strategy and the hierarchy of work and workers it produces helps to simplify things for businesses, employers, and employees, because it makes clear which work is supposedly important enough to a business to be staffed, managed, motivated, and compensated. Also, these categorizations permit businesses to focus on remunerating only certain kinds of work, and permit economists to measure and study only certain kinds of work, instead of considering all kinds of work. The typologies and hierarchies of work are ways to fracture an ecosystem of work and workers into manageable pieces so that some pieces can be maximized for output and profit while other pieces are ignored.

We'll start first with the most macro separation, between productive work and all other work.

Productive and reproductive labor

To understand what's considered work from the perspective of a business, we can go all the way back to the distinction Marx and Engels make between productive and reproductive labor. "Productive" work produces goods in the economy and "reproductive" work reproduces the labor power (aka the workers themselves) required to maintain the economy (Duffy, 2007). While productive labor in the workplace is valued because it creates the surplus value that leads to profits, reproductive labor outside the workplace is also profoundly necessary for a business to generate profit (Hartmann, 1976; Duffy, 2007). It's hard to imagine a productive worker who isn't fed, clothed, and housed somehow.

Feminists expanded the definition of reproductive labor to include:

- Work that renews workers' bodies and energy (e.g., preparing meals and other forms of care),
- Care for people who are not wage workers at the moment (e.g., children who are future wage workers, old people who are no longer wage workers, caretakers who are not themselves wage workers), and
- Work that replaces each generation of workers through childbearing and rearing (Vogel, 2014).

Taking this idea up a notch, feminist theorists considered what employees needed beyond the physical or bodily support to do their jobs. Reproduction is not just physical but also social because individuals, communities, societies, and the economy itself need to reproduce social and political life.

The term "social reproduction" is now used to name various kinds of mental, manual, and emotional work aimed at providing the social and biological care necessary to maintaining existing life and to reproducing the next generation (Laslett and Brenner, 1989). Social reproduction includes processes like teaching and nurturing human beings, leading a family, coordinating human activities, and addressing neighborhood and community needs. Social reproduction also includes organizing sexuality, biological reproduction, how food, clothing, and shelter are made available, and how society is sustained (Ferguson, 2008; Federici, 2012). In addition, social reproduction expansively embraces the work that it takes to become more than we are now, to build better ways of being and living together.

The distinction between production and social reproduction has been used at a macro level by economists to draw the boundaries of business's magic circle. Productive work occurs inside the business and is the business's responsibility, and social reproductive work stays outside the business and is of little or no concern, conventional economists explain. With this separation established, businesses have proceeded to attend only to productive work while failing to attend to any social reproductive work, even the social reproductive work happening within the workplace.

Within the workplace and within jobs themselves, employees perform social reproductive work as well as productive work. So why has the definition of "work" been formally confined to physical labor, rational cognitive calculation, or inspiration, while other forms of real work have been ignored, devalued, and/or made invisible? Because women have disproportionately done this other work, it's so unimportant that it's not really "work" at all.

New types of work identified by feminists

A critical feminist intervention has been to make social reproductive work in the workplace more visible by naming it and explaining why it is valuable (Fletcher, 1998). Some of the most important categories of work that feminists have defined include:

1. Care work – maintaining, supporting, and attending to each other's needs and the needs of our world,
2. Emotional labor – demonstrating and experiencing emotions to facilitate getting work done, and
3. Relational work – demonstrating interpersonal and relationship skills to connect with people to coordinate, execute, and process productive work.

For feminists, raising the profile of caring work, emotional work, and relational work in the workplace has helped not only to value the experiences of women and marginalized people at work, and to provide tools for addressing gendered inequality, but also to challenge the overall marketplace ideology and patriarchal structuring of our understanding of work itself.

1. Care work

Care work is the broadest "new" category of work. Care work

> includes everything we do to maintain, contribute and repair our 'world' so that we can live in it as well as possible. That work includes our bodies, our selves and our environments, all of which we seek to interweave in a complex, life-sustaining web.
>
> (Tronto and Fisher, 1990, p. 40)

From a feminist perspective, care is not just practical, but also relational, emotional, and intimate.

Care can't easily and precisely be distinguished from other kinds of work since nearly all human activity has some element of care work involved. Ultimately, however we categorize these activities, we know that these sorts of work are under-recognized, under-appreciated, under-paid, done by less valued workers, and absolutely critical to business success.

Feminists value care work of all kinds because it fulfills a human need to create, to create conditions that invite growth for ourselves and others, and to care for things outside ourselves. Care and generativity require us to put aside individual self-interest to care about others' needs and group interests. This activity allows us to grow to our highest form of personal maturity and human development (Gilligan, 1982).

It's also true that relationships through which we care for each other (inside or outside the workplace) are ways that we generate meaning, value, love, and intimacy. Caring gives life meaning and helps each of us express our own humanity.

Care work requires that we recognize others' needs and put our own needs second to the needs of those being helped, which violates the self-centeredness encouraged by neoliberalism. Self-sacrificing behavior or even putting someone else's needs ahead of one's own seems illogical – if not outright crazy – in a business environment where coworkers are often also competing with each other.

2. Emotional labor

Emotional labor is a human effort that manages, marshals, musters up, or mimics feelings in the service of work. It includes the work folks do to induce or suppress their feelings so that they can achieve the external demeanor and internal state of mind that's appropriate to the work situations they face (Hochschild, 1983). Emotional labor is also using feelings (one's own or someone else's) to accomplish some goal – to leave a customer satisfied or to get someone to do something they might not otherwise want to. Emotional labor is skilled, effort-intensive, and productive labor. It creates value, improves productivity, and generates profit (Wharton, 2009).

Emotional labor is one of the few academic concepts that has been recruited from the ivory tower into pop culture because everyday folks have found the concept so useful. Finally, there's a way to label and thus see all the extra effort it takes to keep relationships going, to persuade people, to make people feel better, and to feel better yourself in a workplace that can be demanding, stressful, or depleting.

The construct of emotional labor has also been particularly appreciated by women, and by men of color, because it captures what turns out to be an additional burden of work that they have to perform far more often than privileged White men do. For example, women in general often find they must perform emotional labor to behave in "appropriately" feminine ways or to manage the demands of acting more masculine. For Black women, it takes extra work to present an emotional veneer that allows them to fit into a dominant white culture (Durr and Wingfield, 2011). Most people of color find themselves doing emotional work to care for others who are (also) struggling with racism and sexism at work. One colleague told me she spends at least an hour each workday providing "mentorship" – otherwise known as care – to peers of color dealing with hostile work situations. She can't put any of this on her performance review because there's no performance objective related to "helping colleagues cope with micro-aggressions." Moreover, the impact of her work is diffuse – no one notices the employee who's been calmed down and gone back to work, or the team relationship that was repaired before it blew up.

3. Relational work

Relational work (sometimes called "relational practice" [Fletcher, 1999]) is the strategic use of relational skills to do good work and accomplish organizational goals. "High quality connections" (Dutton and Heaphy, 2003) where people recognize and mutually support each other can lead to thriving and flourishing, but they also require nurturing attention. Relational work includes building relationships, managing team dynamics, and resolving conflicts among co-workers. It can even include non-interpersonal work, such as picking up extra tasks to make sure the group's project moves along (Fletcher, 1999). Relational coordination work focuses on dynamics beyond dyadic relationships or team goals (Gittell, 2006), such as attending to the relational health and interdependent productivity of a whole unit of coworkers.

Women and men who take up care work, emotional labor, or relational work often feel like they are doing two jobs – the job they get paid for, and a second job comprised of invisible, taxing, undervalued, and critical forms of work. None of this essential work has been fully appreciated for its contributions to production, to the workplace, and to workers' experiences of work. Instead, these types of work have been ignored, silenced, made invisible or "been disappeared" (Fletcher, 1999) because of the ways they threaten how the status quo defines, values, manages, and rewards "work."

How valuable work is made to disappear

Fletcher's (1999) groundbreaking research on relational work identified specific, genderrelated ways that relational work is rendered invisible to managers, workers, and management scholars. The analyses she offers about relational work also apply to care work, emotional work, and social reproduction work in general.

The work involved in relational, care, emotional, and social reproductive work disappears when people misdiagnose the motive behind it. People often interpret this work as an expression of a worker's personality or, worse, a demonstration of their selfless naiveté. Few recognize that these behaviors can be strategic, intentional enactments of a larger strategic effort to get work done. A second way these kinds of work disappear is when we simply don't have words to describe these additional tasks and explain what they help to accomplish.

For women specifically, a third mode of disappearance occurs when people perceive this behavior not as a worker's deliberate choice about how work could get done, but instead as behavior that just happens because the worker is female. Women's strategic, productively oriented relational practice gets seen as these women "mothering" their coworkers or the project group, rather than recognized as skillful, emotionally intelligent, growth-focused management practice.

Caring work, emotional work, and social reproductive work is actual work requiring time, attention, effort, and skill. This work helps other workers get better at what they do, contributing to a business's profit and its ongoing organizational sustainability. So why can't we recognize these efforts, plain and simple, as legitimate work? Because these forms of work contradict the masculine, patriarchal construction of work and productivity.

These work types privilege mutuality, connection, and interpersonal responsibility, and so they challenge the conventional belief that self-reliance and autonomy are what workers should aspire to. For example, in work cultures that celebrate ambition, competition, and individual promotion, any work done to help someone else be productive can only be explained by assuming the caring worker is weak, or naive, or doing the work out of love for the work or affection for the person/s being helped (or perhaps more cynically, by believing they are helping only somehow to advance their own interests). Similarly, the assertion that individual achievement, heroism, and self-centered rational optimization are what matter to success at work is contradicted when workers attend to the group's process, to mutual relationships, or to each other's needs, and in so doing improve each other's effectiveness at work.

Relational work increases performance, increases collaboration and innovation, and improves group process (Gittell, 2006; Kreeger and Holloway, 2008). But disappearing the work and the intentions behind it makes it impossible to see the very real link between these types of work and overall productivity and effectiveness.

A manager might see that coworkers have good rapport, but fail to see the work that maintains their positive relationships. A manager might also miss how the quality of these relationships drives the quality of the work employees produce individually and together. Without seeing this work and valuing it properly, we've designed our organizations not to facilitate it.

To be sure, as the workplace changes and newer models of collaborative, co-creative, networked, and digital projects have evolved, conventional business has accepted that some emotionality, some relational focus, and maybe even some care work should be valued and supported in the organization. But this support is provisional as well as partial, because of a fourth method through which these types of "not seen as productive work" are disappeared.

Disappearance through selective attention

A language of care and relationship-building has become more prevalent at work (Liedtka, 1996). But, rather than attending to all the situations and employees involved in emotional, relational, and care work, some organizations have paid only selective attention, like the manager who only notices when you win, but not when you try. Businesses seem to cherry-pick the work that feels easiest to assimilate, manage, or marketize while continuing to ignore other work. For example, businesses want employees to demonstrate relational skills that enhance team performance, but businesses still struggle with, ignore, or disappear other types of emotional work, such as the work of supporting a grieving colleague or negotiating the end of a failed client relationship (Worline and Dutton, 2017).

Care work is valued differently depending on who performs it. When women's jobs require caring work, they receive less recognition and are paid less for this work. Men are rated more favorably than women when they help coworkers, while women have to help more just to get the same ratings as men who don't help at all (Heilman and Chen, 2005). For low-wage workers and for women in general, the financial return on their caring skills is largely negative or absent. By contrast, when men's high-wage occupations include care work, men receive a wage premium (Pietrykowski, 2017).

Emotional, relational, and care work that is equally difficult can also vary in perceived importance based on whom it serves. For example, in businesses where clients take priority over coworkers, relational work related to external clients is more important and better supported than relational work focused internally on coworkers. Companies invest time and money managing customer relationships because these are critical to revenue growth. Meanwhile, in-house relationships don't get the same degree of attention, even though internal breakdowns could also damage client relationships (Kreeger and Halloway, 2008).

Some emotional, relational, and care work gets attention, but only if and when it is thought to have some discernible connection to business results. And although care work, emotional labor, and relational work contribute to productivity, productivity isn't the only reason we do it. We value this work because it allows us to feel connected and understood, to mature as adults, and to become fully human. We do this work because it is necessary for life.

Recognizing the care economy

Wrapped around the conventionally defined market economy and providing it critical life support is an ecosystem that feminists call the "care economy." This care economy includes all forms of work and workers involved in care work and social reproduction. Without the care economy, the market economy as we know it cannot function. But like the way ungrateful teens treat adults, the market economy treats the care economy as if it barely existed, and then only with disdain.

The care economy is abused by businesses that refuse to recognize and adequately value all the care work that contributes to their profits and their very survival. Businesses ignore or take advantage of the care they depend on, the work that provides this care, and the people inside and outside their companies who do this work. Inside the organization, work done to care for the organization itself, such as training staff or maintaining the physical plant, is no longer valued enough by many businesses for them to pay their own full-time employees to do it. Instead, businesses "outsource" this work to other companies who can do it more cheaply – largely because they pay their workers lower wages and fewer benefits. The original business gets to save money by paying as little as possible to someone else to do critical care work. Of course, the workers at the outsourcing company are earning less for doing the same work, often part-time and without employee benefits. Meanwhile, inside the business, employees are also doing unpaid care work, emotional labor, and relational work on top of and in addition to the productive work they are being paid for. By thus undervaluing care work, businesses keep their care costs low.

Businesses also take advantage of the care work that their employees' families and networks provide, by encouraging a shift of care responsibilities from well-paid but time-starved employees, to lesser paid workers, to unpaid workers. Think of the employees who work sixty hours a week. There has to be someone doing laundry, buying food, and caring for the children (future employees) on their behalf. Sometimes an unpaid family member will do the work, otherwise the employee will hire lower-waged, lower status people (usually women) to do their care work for them. These hired care workers will pay even lower wages to the babysitters who care for the care worker's children while she works. The downward cascade of care work pays less and less to workers who provide the care that everyone above them in the chain depends upon, all so that every person and business further up the chain gets a little extra surplus value to claim as their own. This "global care chain" (Hochschild, 2000) is how the market economy exploits the less powerful and the more dependent to make a profit.

It's critical to recognize that this care chain starts in the business, where companies pay for only part of the work and some of the workers that contribute to the productivity that generates profit. What looks like a problem of domestic care outside the company is really a problem created by the demands of the businesses, industries, and economy that employ paid workers. Businesses require higher level workers to work too many hours for their salaries, and pay lower level workers too little to cover their own life care.

Here's just one example: when companies pay too little for workers to provide for their own needs and/or they deliberately limit the number of hours employees work to keep from having to pay them employee benefits, these "working poor" employees rely on public assistance programs to meet their basic needs. This practice requires U.S. taxpayers to subsidize businesses about $153 billion per year so that their employees can receive basic life care such as food and housing (UCB Labor Center, 2015). Meanwhile, businesses keep their own labor costs beneath the actual dollar value of the work they receive, by disavowing that they receive anything more than what they pay for.

Business strives to hide the ways it depends on care work because it wants to promote itself as autonomous, independent, and in control. And, by shortchanging the care economy, business can maximize its profits. Capitalism runs on surplus value, on getting people to buy things at prices that are higher than what it costs to produce these things. Businesses can generate more surplus value and more profit by keeping costs low – or not accounting for them at all. Business pushes the care economy outside its magic circle and treats the costs of care work as externalities (Acker, 2004; Folbre, 2006; Fraser, 2016). Care work and social reproduction are the biggest, most complex "off balance sheet" contributors to our economy and to our marketized notion of profits. But imagine what it would be like if businesses took more responsibility for the care and caregivers that it depends on. What if businesses supported more of their employees' life care work? What if businesses paid for more of the care that they receive? What if businesses structured jobs to ensure that employees had enough time in a day to attend to their own care responsibilities?

Re-centering the economy around care

Imagine what it might be like if care was valued, even if only for supporting the marketplace economy. Even better, imagine what it might it be like to work with, work for, manage within, and transact with customers as a business that – despite its dependence on others or their dependence on us – sees customers as people who need care that our business would be honored to provide? Imagine how that would change pricing, marketing, purchasing, and collaboration.

Feminists want business to shift our notion of "the economy" from a focus on the marketplace to a focus on caring. Feminists believe that human beings are *Homines curans* – an explicitly plural, collective, "caring people" (Folbre, 2006; Tronto, 2017). Because care is the foundation of human life, care – and not production, transactions, or profits – should drive how we organize our collective project. To center care, we could, for example, rethink how productive work and life care work should be distributed among people, businesses, and other social institutions. Life care work shouldn't be dumped onto the lowest valued workers. Instead, it should be equitably distributed among all people because everyone needs the chance that caring work provides to build the relationships of nurturance, love, care, and solidarity that help us become fully human (Lynch, Baker, and Lyons, 2009). The workplace would become a place where everyone has the chance to learn, to grow, and to contribute in both mundane and meaningful ways.

In a marketplace economy, the separation of productive work and life care work makes it hard for us to participate in work as full human beings. Our current marketplace logic separates productive work from life care work, and then positions productive work as "more valuable." This encourages and even drives people to focus their lives on productive work (that provides wages, and in our culture, social status) in ways that add to profits, but not necessarily to workers' lives. The all-consuming demands of productive work lead people to diminish, distance, or even separate themselves from social reproductive work. Yet, it's this very same life care work that provides people's lives with meaning and each other's lives with the care they cannot live without. By structuring our lives and society around production, a market-only economy estranges us from our chances to be fully human. That's why a market-only economy is so socially destructive. It prevents us and everyone else from flourishing.

Given that life care and production are intertwined, it is impossible to achieve gender equality within the productive systems of business without also changing how we manage the caring economy that wraps around and reaches inside business. We can't get equality in businesses unless we also address gendered inequality in the care economy. We should address these "externalities" by re-incorporating processes of care into our understanding of economics and business. Until we transform our economic, social, and political practices into caring practices, we cannot really hope to live democratically as equals where everyone has the same potential to flourish.

This is not a utopian vision. Rather, it's a priority that brings into focus what human life is really about. Centering care escorts the market economy and its legitimating ideology out from its central role in shaping our priorities and guiding our actions. It also removes business and work from its dominion over our culture, our family lives, and our self-definition. We can begin to center care by imagining a business where all forms of necessary work are valued, and where we prioritize not the profits of the business's owners or even everyone's life care activity, but living itself.

Work–family–life conflict

No popular conversation about women in the workplace gets more attention than the conversation about work and family. With women responsible for the unpaid social reproduction work in the home and community, how can women balance their family responsibilities with the demands of a "real" job?

This question is raised over and over, and it always points to the wrong place. It keeps asking women how they can manage these competing demands, instead of asking businesses why women should have to.

Originally known as the "work–family" dilemma, this tension between work and the rest of life was imagined as a conflict between women's paid work and their social, reproductive, family work. More recently, feminists have broadened the scope of the conversation to include "work–family–life," so that it incorporates not only the concerns of mothers or parents, but also the concerns of any worker interested in having a life beyond the workplace. Thinking about "work–life" tensions also helps to include the families and communities that are affected when employees struggle with competing demands.

The current conversation about work–family–life isn't about making sure that employees, their families, and their communities can accomplish both productive paid labor and the social reproductive activities their lives depend on. It isn't even about gender equality, although it pretends to be both these things. Work–life conversations focus on finding ways to accommodate employees' social reproduction needs with the least possible disturbance of "business as usual."

Adjustments around the margins of business as usual have given some employees paid time off, personal days, parental leave, and other tools for temporarily reducing the tensions that businesses create for employees. Businesses have also adjusted some day-to-day expectations of employees, offering remote work, job-sharing, part-time work, and mommy tracks. These efforts have helped some employees wrap duct tape around their work and life responsibilities to hold things together, and employees have appreciated these changes.

And yet, despite decades of discussion, analysis, and pilot programs, businesses still haven't addressed feminism's most significant critique: it is business's own conventions of job design, pay scales, and work schedules that create the work–life problems that businesses tell individual employees to solve.

To enable work–life balance for employees, business will need to address these six issues:

1. *Businesses deny the demands of biology, treat female pregnancy as an aberrant exception, and use nature as an excuse to avoid dealing with sexism.*
Work organizations remain designed around a fully able-bodied male, and even then work and work-time expectations often push this ideal worker to unhealthy lengths. The presumption of an always able (male) worker makes it impossible for most women ever to fit without accommodation. Let's take just one simple example: pregnancy and childbirth. Consider that since a third of women in the paid workforce are mothers, with an average of two children each (US Dept. of Labor, 2016), businesses can expect employees to have more than one child, and need to manage deaths, illnesses, childcare, and elder care expectations. Yet, only 15 percent of U.S. workers have access to paid family leave (Bureau of Labor Statistics, 2016) and at many companies, even maternity leaves that are unpaid are offered begrudgingly. To be able to interrupt work and lose income so that she can give birth without threatening her livelihood remains a privilege for some working women and an impossibility for most others. Moreover, pregnancy is still often treated as a temporary handicap, with an employee's disability benefits paying a portion of the salary she loses while recovering from childbirth. Maternity leave is even described as "taking time off," as though giving birth is like going on vacation. This despite proof, over millennia, that procreation is a completely normal, predictable, and profoundly human activity.

If our businesses are designed in ways that make it a problem when employees participate in this critical element of humanity, there's something wrong. And businesses can fix it.

But they don't. Instead of redesigning work systems to fit predictable phases of human life, businesses build a pattern of workplace discrimination against mothers called the "maternal wall" (Williams, 2004). Maternal wall discrimination includes holding mothers to higher performance standards than men, giving mothers returning from their maternity leave less desirable assignments than they held before they had children, and assuming that having a baby makes a woman "less competent, less committed, less suitable for hire, promotion and management training, and deserving of lower salaries" (Correll, Benard, and Paik, 2007, p. 1320).

Coworkers also interpret the behavior of colleagues who are mothers through a maternal lens. A man who is absent is assumed to be on a sales trip or sick with the flu, while a woman who is absent is assumed to be taking care of her children. And even before they have babies, "visibly pregnant women managers are judged (by managers) as less committed to their jobs, less dependable, and less authoritative, but warmer, more emotional, and more irrational than otherwise equal women managers who are not visibly pregnant" (Correll, Benard, and Paik, 2007, p. 1298).

This maternal wall of bias translates into a concrete, objective decrease in income known as the motherhood penalty (Budig and England, 2001) of about 5 percent per child (Kricheli-Katz, 2012). Meanwhile, men who become fathers experience a financial and career boost. They are more likely to be hired than childless men. And once they have children, the fatherhood bonus increases men's salaries by more than 6 percent (Budig, 2014).

The big picture presumptions that build the maternal wall are that (1) women who have children are seen as likely to downshift or opt out and thus aren't worth a company's investment as workers, and (2) almost every female is expected to eventually become a mother, so why even take a chance on women employees, given the odds? (Kossek, Su, and Wu, 2017). Of course, it's not the women who are the problem – becoming a mother is normal. It's not something women can change so that they fit better with business's expectations. What can change, though, is the way that businesses design jobs, careers, and schedules.

2. Work–family–life issues show that businesses are unable or unwilling to address questions of equity and justice.
Both businesses and employees confine their conversations about work–life to questions of formal equality. They aim to treat everyone the same, regardless of the inequalities this creates in outcomes. Formal equality makes sense where an employee's sex, race, age, etc. makes no material difference. However, formal equality doesn't work where male and female employees really do differ, such as pregnancy and childbirth. Employers are reluctant to take an equity approach and offer programs designed for the specific needs of one group of employees and not others, because they don't want to be seen as treating employees differently. Businesses seem unable to find a way to treat pregnant women both differently and equitably, and to develop a confident response if another group mislabels this as "preferential" treatment (Williams, 1991).

The basic design of too many businesses and too many career paths makes formal equality impossible. If getting promoted to managing director means devoting oneself to 60 plus-hour work weeks for the first ten years of one's career, say between ages 24 and 35, the promotion track is designed deliberately to exclude women who get pregnant and must take time away from paid work to complete their pregnancies and recover from giving birth. Businesses have yet to consider a justice-oriented approach that would have them eliminate what's causing the barriers to equal outcomes and equal contributions. If career paths and job roles were rejigged, if work time expectations were reduced, the obstacles for women, mothers, parents, and others with family responsibilities would be lowered dramatically and work–life issues would be more manageable for everyone.

3. *The design of business ignores employees' life responsibilities and leaves little room for social reproduction because it starves us of time.*

Looking more broadly, beyond pregnancy and childbirth, work–life conflict is endemic, salient, and serious for nearly everyone because work and business are currently organized to deny employees' life responsibilities. Everyone has some responsibility for social reproductive work. Everyone has a body that needs to be cared for. Every adult needs some outlet for nurturing to become fully human (Gilligan, 1982). The design of work to be all-consuming causes work–life problems because it imagines that these basic human needs don't exist, don't need any significant time, or just aren't that important when compared to wage-earning and careers. Business positions itself as more important, more worthy, and more deserving of time than these other life elements. Yet, everyone needs time and energy to create and continue life, to have families and friends, and to participate in communities. The world of work and business simply cannot give us all that we need to be fully human, and we can't get it from the rest of life if we have no time.

Treating the work–life tension as something to be fixed by "balancing" asks us to indulge in an unrealistic fantasy: we'd have enough time and energy for all of it, if we could only juggle our schedules a little better, and maybe if employers gave us the flexibility to make adjustments around the edges. People can't find a healthy equilibrium between work time and social life time when work consumes the lion's share of time and still bites into what remains of our time outside of work.

Too many employees, parents or not, already struggle to maintain their lives and social reproductive activity outside of work in the face of long commutes, demanding jobs, schedules that defy the need for rest, and work weeks that swallow up their waking hours. Employees are relatively powerless to change the terms of work because working less than "full time" usually means not earning enough money to live on. Of course, workers "manage" as best they can, but managing scarce resources is not the same as giving self, family, and community enough time to flourish.

Productive work (e.g., paid employment) and social reproductive work (e.g., family care) are inextricably bound together. The "separation" is only conceptual, allowing us to imagine them as independent spheres of decision-making that occasionally conflict with each other. That's like saying exhaling has nothing to do with how much you inhale when they are both parts of the same process of breathing. Yet by proceeding as if what happens at work has no bearing on what happens outside of work, businesses ignore any responsibility for what employees are dealing with in their lives because of these extreme work demands (Gascoigne, Parry, and Buchanan, 2015). Instead, businesses emphasize individual responsibilities and options for resolving work–family conflict, while ignoring calls for significant change in how business organizes itself (Padavic, Ely, and Reid, 2018). Businesses style themselves as responsive good guys, helping employees manage work–life conflicts that employees' own life choices have created, even though it's businesses themselves who benefit from the demands they make of employees.

4. Blaming employees for life choices: family is employees' choice, balance is employees' responsibility.

To avoid their responsibility for work–family tensions, businesses encourage us to define work–life problems and solutions not as organizational, political, economic, or cultural issues, but as the result of individual "choices." Women choose to become mothers, fathers choose to want to have relationships with their kids, and people choose to want nourishing meals after work. When family and life needs are framed as the result of personal choices, rather than as regular, predictable, and normal expectations for human life, we treat them differently.

The belief that motherhood is a choice provides employers in America with a superficially legitimate reason to discriminate against mothers (Gascoigne, Parry, and Buchanan, 2015). If we believe that a certain situation is controllable, then we are more likely to view people who suffer from these circumstances as responsible, to judge, reject, and dislike them, and to treat them negatively. This is why when motherhood is shaped as a "choice", as a self-centered decision that could be controlled or avoided, employers and coworkers feel more comfortable judging mothers and making mothers themselves responsible for their work–life conflicts. Of course, these mothers are indeed "choosing" to work and earn wages. They could "choose" to opt out from paid work and not to earn an income, although that would be hard on the 25 percent of families headed by a sole female breadwinner (Department of Labor, 2016).

When we believe that people can choose a mommy track, or choose an unpaid maternity leave, or choose to leave work to pick up a sick child, we are more likely to judge them to be lacking if they can't keep it all together. They become less-than-ideal workers as well as less-than-ideal parents. We're urged to forget that having children is a contribution to the social good. But shouldn't it matter to all of us that children are brought into the world and lovingly cared for as they grow?

Employees can choose to request work–life accommodations in companies that offer them, but having to ask is difficult for workers. Employees rightly fear that asking for accommodations is tantamount to saying that they actually can't do the job as designed. And, since companies can't have every associate manager out on maternity leave or working from home all at once, managers have to coordinate employees' use of work–life accommodations. Concerns about interfering with the business's overall productivity lead managers to use their discretion, and their biases, when they permit accommodations. Employees then have to compete with each other to get the accommodation they need. Competition is tight when employees perceive that benefits are scarce or unevenly awarded, as well as when they believe that one employee's accommodation ends up burdening other employees with more work.

Employees have reason to be concerned, because opportunities for work–life benefits aren't evenly distributed throughout most organizations (Kelliher and Anderson, 2010). Even among the upper echelon professional employees who are offered work–life benefits, this opportunity is available only to the most privileged. Only certain people will be able to work hard enough and well enough to be considered by their companies as worth the extra cost of work–life accommodations. Many employees feel the need to prove themselves worthy of these benefits, often by working even more (Kelliher and Anderson, 2010). For example, women on maternity leave participate in conference calls while nursing their newborns. This extra work perversely increases employees' strain, and also increases their contributions to the business. An employee has to be an ideal worker to deserve benefits, but once benefits are used it becomes impossible for them to be an ideal worker ever again. Too many employees lack predictable and reasonable working hours that might make these policies unnecessary, and too many lack job security that make it possible to advocate for their own and their coworkers' needs.

Are there real options for eliminating work–life tension?

At the root of the work–life conversation is a truth too many businesses can't or won't hear: it's not the balance between work and family, or the rigidity or flexibility of work schedules, or the presence or absence of pregnant workers that's causing the problems that employees experience. It's the unceasing demand for more work and more time at work that has pushed employees to their limits. It's that one salary from one decent job doesn't pay enough to allow employees to sustain themselves and their families. The real issues here are not women's childcare responsibilities or employees' need to contribute to social reproduction. The real issues are overwork and inadequate pay.

If companies designed jobs that didn't demand so much of employees' time and energy, employees would have much more leeway to accomplish both wage work and life care work. More time away from work would certainly reduce work–life stress. This is not to say that shorter work days and work weeks would solve every work–life problem (e.g., it wouldn't necessarily solve maternity leave), but a significant number of work and life stresses would disappear if employers demanded less time from each employee (and perhaps hired a few more employees to spread the work around) (Schultz and Hoffman, 2006). Redesigning jobs and work to make them more humane doesn't need to hurt a business's profits or threaten its financial stability. Businesses could follow the lead of companies like Basecamp, makers of project and client management software. With its "calm company" initiative, Basecamp combines its emphasis on profitability with protecting people's time and attention, having reasonable productivity expectations, and keeping work within 40 hours a week for everyone from the CEO to entry-level developers (Fried and Hansson, 2018). Basecamp has found that employees' investment in creating a business-wide strategy for making work efficient and leaving plenty of room for the rest of life has helped to keep the business profitable and growing.

In addition to redesigning work weeks to be closer to 35 hours than to 55, businesses could also take an approach that directly addresses justice to reshape jobs and career paths according to the principles of inclusive design. Inclusive design considers the full range of human diversity when designing something to consider at the very beginning how to make a task, job, or career ladder that would work for anyone, regardless of sex, parenting and family status, and so on. Inclusive design recognizes that our needs shift with time and circumstance, so it anticipates different ways an individual might interact with the workplace as life goes on. It's not about making exceptions for some people, such as offering a professional woman an additional year on the male-defined partner track when she has a child. Job designers would seek to create the "curb-cut effect," where something designed for the most challenged group of workers ends up creating ease for everyone (curb-cuts on sidewalks intended for wheelchair users also help bicyclists, parents with strollers, delivery people, and more). Inclusive design would restructure work days, weeks, and years so that employees who face the most predictable human challenges can handle them smoothly.

Instead of blaming employees because they don't fit a poorly designed work system, businesses could change the work system. Then, employees' contributions could be less influenced by how well or poorly they fit the male model of the ideal worker.

At the same time, each wage-earner could be compensated more adequately for the work that they do and the contributions they make. Consider that between 1973 and 2017 employees' productivity has grown 6.2 times more than their pay (Economic Policy Institute, 2018). Although employees are more productive than ever, the wealth their work has generated has gone disproportionately to owners, shareholders, and top managers rather than being shared with all employees. If employees were simply paid a larger share of the profits they help to earn, many households would no longer need two full-time wage-earners to make ends meet. Two-parent families could decide how to divide one full-time paid job and one full-time home job, and heads of single-earner households would make enough to afford fairly paid domestic help, yet still have more hours in the week to be with their families. Hearkening back to the idea of a family wage, but without the presumption that it be paid to men to support their women, a right-sized full-time job at a sustaining wage would give households the financial resources, time, and energy to approach work as a support for their full lives.

Making these changes would require all of us to reframe the ways that we think about work and life. First, we'd shift to prioritize life over work, so that instead of "living to work" we would work to help ourselves and others flourish in life. This reordering would not mean dissing work or taking advantage of our jobs or employees, but rather transforming how we see the relationship between work and life. We'd replace the framing that imagines separation and conflict with a frame that imagines integration and mutual benefit. We would understand the role of work not as the centerpiece of our lives, but as a way to support flourishing lives.

Gendered work, gendered wages

Articles about the gendered segregation of jobs, occupations, and managerial levels usually start with the same paragraph – a long list of data points showing how women are disproportionately in lower levels of organizations, in less prestigious and less remunerative occupations, and in less glamorous jobs. I'll spare you this paragraph. All you need to prove that women and men are disproportionately clustered doing different work, different jobs, and different occupations is a quick look around you.

What you might not see, though, is the gendering of work, jobs, and occupations that creates this visibly unbalanced relationship between gender and jobs. Look closely at a list of job postings and you'll see that some of these jobs are colored blue, like firefighting, data science, and manufacturing, while other jobs like retail clerk, customer service, or kindergarten teaching are pink pink pink. You'll also see that every job with a blue tinge is more important, preferred, and better paid. In contrast, any job that's pink is helpful, complementary, or subservient, requiring lots of relational skills and caretaking, but poorly paid. It's less desirable and less important.

Work, jobs, and occupations are blue or pink, gendered masculine or feminine, and everything is valued or debased according to this gendering. And woe to those who are gender non-conforming or transgender, because they fit nowhere in this world of blue and pink work.

Whether it is the result of outright discrimination (yes), gender-specific sexist social expectations (yes), sexist opportunity structures and pathways from school to career (yes), or personal preferences tinged by sexist self-assessments (yes), occupational segregation causes problems for gender equality.

Why care about gendered segregation in business?

Four important reasons why business should be concerned with work segregation by gender include (Hesmondhalgh and Baker, 2015):

1. Gender segregation is strongly linked to inequality. Jobs and occupations performed by women tend to be paid less than those done by men.

2. Work segregation by gender limits the autonomy, freedom, and recognition accorded to individual women and men. When a person has talents that would help them thrive in a particular occupation, but that occupation's gender doesn't match their own, they are much less likely to pursue that occupation, thus limiting their chance of success.

3. Work segregation by gender draws upon, and in turn contributes to, social stereotypes that reinforce the problem of gendered occupational segregation.

4. Work segregation by gender limits collective flourishing, because it makes it harder for people to match their talents to occupations, thus inhibiting the ways people's talents might serve the common good.

Most people realize that vertical segregation is not caused by men being better at management than women. Instead, they understand the cause to be mostly sexism with a smidgen of personal choice. Common metaphors of the "glass ceiling" and "glass pyramid" express our cultural understanding that patriarchy creates invisible barriers that increase gendered inequality as men and women rise or fail to rise up a company's power structure.

Where we do need help to see gendered dynamics is when we turn to horizontal segregation – where women and men can be found clustered in different kinds of work, jobs, and occupations. Horizontal segregation is thought to be a "more benign division" (Cohen, 2013) because it seems like something women and men choose because they prefer different kinds of work, and not the result of sexism. Regardless of how we get there, horizontal segregation is detrimental to gender equality because it affects the earnings, career mobility, and work autonomy of just about every employed woman or person, as well as the fortunes of everyone who depends on these wage-earners. It reinforces cultural gender stereotypes in society, makes the labor market less flexible and less efficient, and under-utilizes too many people's skills and talents. It is also the main driver of the gendered wage gap.

Horizontal segregation is organized by the ways that skills, tasks, jobs, roles, and occupations are gendered. When we look closely, we can see the socially constructed links between the work itself, the gender of the skills and talents needed to do the work, and the gender of the people who best fit (and best perform) these kinds of skills. Recall that to sustain "gender," we have to believe that men and women have essentially different qualities and that these different qualities lead them to be better (or worse) at some kinds of work than at other kinds (Alvesson and Billing, 2002). Because businesses want to fill jobs with the people who can best perform them, gendered jobs are filled most of the time by people whose gender matches that job. When "data scientist" is seen as male/masculine, people look for men to fill that job, just as they look for women to fill the female/feminine job of "editorial assistant."

You may wonder what happens with men or women who don't fit heterosexist norms. Research suggests that gay men seem to fit equally well into masculine or feminine jobs (Clarke and Arnold, 2018). Both gay men and lesbians tend to seek occupations where they can work independently or use their social perceptiveness, since these are strategies that help them manage the stigma they might anticipate from homophobia and heterosexism (Tilcsik, Anteby, and Knight, 2015).

The gendering of jobs, skills, and tasks is driven by broad gender stereotypes of masculinity and femininity. Feminine/female/women's occupations all entail job characteristics that include caring for others, while masculine/male/men's occupations are more production-oriented and focused on things rather than relationships. In another cyclical chicken-and-egg interaction, jobs thought to require masculine qualities are predominantly staffed with men, and when men are the majority of employees in a job, that job is gendered as masculine/male. Those "blue collar" and "pink collar" jobs you see get created by sorting men into some work and women into other work.

Gendering of jobs is fundamentally arbitrary, and it harms both women and men. A study of bank workers in a newly created role demonstrated that the same role could be gendered as either masculine or feminine (Doering and Thébaud, 2017). When men originated these roles, their clients gendered the role as masculine, while when women originated these roles, their clients gendered the role as feminine. Moreover, in the very same role, men in the masculine-gendered version were able to wield substantially more authority over clients than women in the feminine-gendered version. The gender of the role-holder influenced how the job was gendered and what level of authority the job was seen to have.

Because most jobs contain elements that can be easily categorized as either masculine and feminine, any gender can be assigned to any given job – and even switch over time. In the 1890s, secretarial work was a well-paid stepping stone to management, and it was performed overwhelmingly by men. Men were supposedly terrific at tasks required of a secretary, such as managing the complex schedule of an important person. Now, that very same work is seen to be a better fit with women, since women are supposedly terrific at managing the complex schedule of an important person. Same requirements, differently gendered, and with one additional twist: when secretarial work became women's work, it was no longer seen as a stepping stone to a higher position (Pringle, 1993).

Gendering drives power, status, and wages

Work that carries power and influence is seen to require qualities associated with men, while work lacking power and authority becomes associated with women (Ely and Padavic, 2007). Men move into high-value professions while women are disproportionately herded into unstable, low-wage occupations. And even when women break into male-dominated occupations, they often get shunted into less prestigious work and roles within these occupations. Given the current emphasis on getting "women in tech," consider this example of how work within an occupation becomes gendered. In the field of computer engineering, work roles are often split (consciously and unconsciously) into binary, oppositional types of "technical work" and "social work." Technical work includes creating and using tools for practical purposes, a form of "masculine instrumentalism" (Faulkner, 2000). Opposite this technical work is interpersonal work that includes communication, creating relationships, and managing the emotions of tool use, a form of "feminine expressiveness." Non-technical elements of work are deemed feminine and thus not understood as "real" engineering.

This separation replicates a gendered hierarchy, a division of labor, that separates who can and cannot do different jobs. Within engineering, patterns of sex segregation and gendered wage allocation map consistently onto this distinction between "technical" and "social" engineering subfields and work activities (Cech, 2013), with women being clustered in the social engineering subfields. Why else are so many of female software engineers found in "front end" work like user interaction and web page interface design that directly connects to consumers, while more male software engineers do "back end" development using machine languages? It's one thing to get women into tech, and another thing entirely to get women into "real" engineering.

When men move into fields that have been gendered as feminine, they often get sorted into the more prestigious jobs in these fields. Then, men enjoy the "glass escalator effect," where men rise disproportionately to the top managerial levels in their field. That's how men come to make up 25 percent of teachers, 48 percent of school principals, and 76 percent of school superintendents (Superville, 2016).

Meanwhile, women who enter occupations that are gendered masculine and dominated by men are punished when they violate gendered expectations of women (Heilman and Okimoto, 2007). Women are disliked for promoting themselves (Rudman, 1998), seen as less hirable, penalized when they negotiate for higher pay (Bowles, Babcock, and Lai, 2007), and lose much of whatever status they have been granted when they show anger (Brescoll and Uhlmann, 2008). Finally, when the gender composition of occupations shift from men to women, average pay declines in response (Levanon, England, and Allison, 2009), a phenomenon known as occupational gender devaluation (Reskin, 1988). Even for general managerial roles across occupations, the movement of more women into management positions has been accompanied by a downgrading of the role of (middle) management itself (Calás and Smircich, 1993).

Many would argue that occupational segregation occurs by choice

The most common explanation for gendered occupational patterns is that women (and men) create it voluntarily through their job and career choices, as if there were no sexism and no gendered differences in power and agency to influence their choices. It's just personal preference that keeps women from pursuing prestigious jobs that pay well, which absurdly suggests that women don't want to be valued and paid for their work. Several mechanisms are proposed to explain occupational segregation, and none of them is more than two steps away from the influence of sexism. These mechanisms include:

1. *Different priorities*: women and men simply have different priorities that they're pursuing through paid work. Women supposedly prioritize creativity and the chance for relationships, men prioritize prestige and earning power. This begs the question of where women and men get these priorities, and why the priorities are patterned by gender rather than by other criteria like personality.

2. *Planning ahead for families*: supposedly, women and men choose jobs and careers with their anticipated parenting and family demands front of mind. This argument explains very few choices, since a recent study of graduating college students found that just 25 percent of men deliberately considered future "provider" responsibilities and merely 13 percent of women considered their potential future caregiver roles when they chose their careers (Cech, 2015).

3. *No skills/no interest*: women and men might also choose jobs and careers based on their assessment of a match between their own skills and talents and those required by a particular job or career, a kind of typecasting. But how do women and men learn about their talents and skills? From their own self-assessment and from feedback that they get from others about what they do well, which may end up reinforcing gendered expectations.

4. *Self-expression and doing what you love*: the idea that people take jobs to maximize their self-expression seems to validate the idea of independent choices. People forget that what we choose and like – and even how we define the self we want to express – is heavily influenced by socialization and cultural expectations, which are gendered themselves (Cech, 2013).

5. *Assessing the likelihood of career success*: women and men are also influenced in their choice of jobs and fields by assumptions about whether they can succeed in a career. Feminists argue that gender-essentialist views push women toward jobs traditionally done by women and push men to stay in male-dominated fields (Correll, 2001). Women see themselves as less likely to succeed in careers that are stereotypically masculine (Barbulescu and Bidwell, 2013) and data show that they aren't wrong.

Gendering wages

Imagine a world where there was no gendered bias and no sexism. We'd see the same proportion of women entering a career as succeeding to its pinnacle roles, from line manager up to CEO. We'd see the same proportion of women and men in high status, socially desirable and high-paying careers. We'd even see more equality in who's burdened by precarious labor and poverty, rather than having women dominate both categories. We'd see women and men in similar jobs, and women and men doing different work at the same level of challenge, being paid equally well.

But we don't have this. Instead, we have not only jobs that are gendered, but also wages that are gendered.

The gendered wage gap is everywhere, in businesses of all sizes and types. The gendered wage gap, roughly speaking, shows that women on average earn 80 percent of what men in comparable jobs earn (NWLC, 2016). When we look at specific groups of women, especially by race/ethnicity, we note that there are additional penalties for women of color, who earn less than White women's 79 percent (it's the Asian women's 87 percent rate that pulls up the average for women overall). The standard for comparison is the most privileged group, White men. However, within the same racioethnic minority group, men earn substantially more than women of the same race (IWPR, 2015).

Even if all possible concrete explanations were taken into account, if women and men had the same education and experience, race, occupation, and so on, the "adjusted" wage for women would rise to only about 91% of men's wages (Blau and Kahn, 2007). While we can't address every possible explanation for the gendered wage gap here, consider that economists and management academics agree that a significant percentage of the gap is likely due to discrimination and unconscious bias (Blau and Kahn, 2007). The finding remains: women and men do not have wage parity.

One critical reason for the gendered wage gap is that the fields in which women work offer them lower pay. This doesn't mean that women "choose" lower paying jobs and men choose higher paying ones. Rather, the jobs that women traditionally do are almost always valued less than men's. According to the Institute for Women's Policy Research, the 20 jobs dominated by women are low-earning ones. These professions, including housekeeping, secretarial work, nursing, and school-teaching, may be paid less because they're seen as "emotional" and "caring" occupations rather than truly "skilled." Women's work, in other words, is circumscribed by social expectations, and then not properly valued. Four of the most common occupations for women have, on average, a below-poverty-line wage for women, and it's substantially worse for women of color (IWPR, 2015).

If you think the gendered wage gap would disappear when women "choose better-paying jobs" or "develop the right skills," consider that switching occupations won't solve the gendered wage gap. Even in the same field or with the similar skills, women aren't compensated equally to their male peers (recall, too, that wages drop when women enter a field previously dominated by men). The gender wage gap is higher in occupations with a higher proportion of women and lower in occupations with more men, but still is found everywhere (Hegewisch, Phil, and Ellis, 2015).

On the other side of the equation, there are business-centered explanations for the gendered wage gap, such as bias in formal hiring and pay systems, as well as managerial bias. Some wage discrimination is overt and intentional, while other practices are the result of unconscious biases and stereotypes (Ridgeway, 2011). When managers have discretion over salaries and bonuses, they can be influenced by their own values and biases. Studies have found that in settings where managers have leeway over rewards and careers, their personal political beliefs influence whether or not they pay men and women the same (Briscoe and Joshi, 2017).

Gender bias is also built into pay and performance systems because these systems rarely establish comparable worth across different jobs. Comparable worth is the idea that jobs requiring similar skill, effort, and importance should be compensated at similar rates. Even where women and men do similar but different jobs (e.g., hotel maids and hospital janitors), the fact that these jobs require the same skills means they should be paid the same. But hotel maids (predominantly women) earn on average $11.84 while janitors (predominantly men) earn $13.41 (U.S. Dept. of Labor, 2017), even though they both change sheets and mop floors. Comparable worth is difficult to assess while men and women are still valued differently.

Obviously, feminists believe it's only fair that women be paid equally to men in similar jobs and in the same jobs. Human lives are at stake, since poverty among working women and their families in the U.S. would be reduced by 51 percent if in all occupations women were paid equal to men (IWPR, 2016).

Feminists also believe that all forms of work that employees contribute to a business's effectiveness should be compensated with fair wages that reflect how business depend on all this work, not just some of it. While feminists acknowledge that pay differences could reflect real differences in the expertise and effort that different forms of work might require, the vast disparities across jobs and occupations along with the pay differentials from the bottom to the top jobs in a company can't be explained by expertise and effort, or even by the supply of workers with abilities that fit these jobs. Indeed, the feminist analyses of gendered work and gendered wages call into question almost all of the assumptions and biases that have established such disparate compensation for different kinds of indispensable work.

If no work were gendered, if the gendered wage gaps were eliminated, if all forms of work were paid for, and if all workers were paid a life-sustaining wage for a full but not overwhelming work week, not just women but all workers and their dependents would have the financial means to support their flourishing.

Foundations of organizational structure

All organizations struggle with tensions between autonomy and coordination, standardization and innovation, centralization and local authority, process and outcomes, and hierarchy and lateral relationships. These tensions are managed through organizational structure. Organizational structure is the interconnected system of routines of behavior, the patterns of interaction, and the flows of communication and resources that compose a scaffolding to support an organization's purpose. Organizational structure includes formal systems for controlling and coordinating tasks and employees, for assigning responsibilities and authority, for concentrating or dispersing decision-making, and for standardizing activities and roles.

Feminists pay attention to how organizational structures build relationships among members, allocate resources, allot participation rights, bind members' autonomy, and establish members' relative importance. Feminists have critiqued features of common organizational structures such as hierarchy, centralization of power, and especially non-democratic governance and decision-making (Anderson, 2017), all of which make inequality predictable and flourishing impossible.

Most businesses are fundamentally unequal and inhumane because our current organizations are not structured in ways that promote human flourishing (Notter and Grant, 2011). They're built for productivity and profit. As long as productivity and profit alone are prioritized, the full humanity of the people doing the work is easy to disregard. If current organizations are rife with gender inequity and obstacles to flourishing, it's because conventional businesses are designed to ignore them or to benefit from them. If organizations want to pursue equality and flourishing, they must have new and different structures.

The feminist critique of bureaucracy

Feminists have long criticized the common organizational structure characterized by specialized functions and jobs, adherence to fixed rules, rationality, objectivity, and a hierarchy of authority, known as bureaucracy (Ferguson, 1984; Iannello, 1992). Describing bureaucracy as the "scientific organization of inequality" (Ferguson, 1984), feminists have argued that the very nature of bureaucracy oppresses women (Ashcraft, 2001) and thwarts flourishing.

In The Feminist Case Against Bureaucracy (1984), Ferguson argues that bureaucracy perpetuates sexism and gender inequality because it (1) relies on steep hierarchies and rigid divisions of labor that formalize inequalities between members; (2) overemphasizes technical qualifications and rationality; and (3) marginalizes social skills, relationships, and emotionality. Bureaucracy not only replicates power relations between women and men outside of the workplace, but also relies on these gender dynamics to help reinforce the organization's own power structures. Bureaucracies also double down on oppression by creating additional patterns of dominating and subordinating to exert control over employees.

Ferguson argues, for example, that bureaucracy disguises the adversarial relations between workers, bosses, owners, and directors by using the anodyne language of administration and markets. Any language of politics that might betray these power dynamics is avoided. Similarly, she notes how the power enshrined in bureaucratic structures often results in employees' pain. "Bureaucracies have a tremendous capacity to hurt people, to manipulate, twist, and damage human possibility" (1984, p. xii). Because bureaucracies are anti-flourishing, they are anti-feminist.

In response to technological changes and to criticisms from feminists, we have seen a wave of more flexible, leaner, less formal organizational forms. In these post-bureaucratic organizations (Alvesson and Thompson, 2006), decisions are more often based on dialogue and consensus rather than authority and command, the organization is more like a network than a hierarchy, boundaries and membership are more fluid, and decision-making is guided more by principles than by rules.

One would imagine these less bureaucratic organizations would be more likely to support feminist values and practice. Alas, many negative aspects of classic bureaucracy have remained, while other aspects have become informal, implicit features rather than formal, explicit ones. For example, nimble, networked organizations like Google might have digital communications and open plan offices that encourage greater collaboration and more democratic ways of working, but they also still have underlying structures of authority and privilege, including chains of command, large salary differentials, and uneven access to decision-making. As Kunda (2006) explained, "the essence of bureaucratic control – the formalization, codification and enforcement of rules and regulations – does not change in principle ... it shifts focus from organizational structure to the organization's culture" (p. 220).

Feminist organizational design alternatives

Feminists discovered this same problematic shift from formal to informal inequalities in their own organizational experiments. Wanting to avoid the illegitimate, unsanctioned power dynamics of hierarchies and aiming to increase participation and agency among members, feminists experimented with organizations that were entirely consensus-driven and/or had very little formal assignment of responsibilities. These organizations were well-intentioned but often unproductive, and many of these early experiments imploded (Riger, 1994). In the feminist classic "The Tyranny of Structurelessness", Jo Freeman (1972) explored what happened when feminist organizations abjured hierarchy (and structure more generally). She found that in the absence of conventional structures or years of experience with alternative coordination practices, informal forms of oppression would arise. For example, the status that some women derived from their wealth and/or their whiteness would give them authority over less privileged women and men in the organization. These informal structures were less effective, less democratic, and less feminist than members wanted.

Feminist organizations challenged themselves to create "flatter" structures with a hierarchy that was legitimate and more limited (Wheeler and Chin, 1991; Iannello, 1992). They created more horizontal, peer-to-peer, relational methods of mutual coordination (Follett, 1924; Koen, 1984) organized less like pyramids and more like networks. These structures, which Helgesen (1995) calls "webs of inclusion," reflect feminist values of agency, equality, collaboration, shared decision-making, and participation, and allow for the creation of community (Gilligan, 1982).

In addition to imagining a different overall structure, feminist organizations also created different building blocks of practices and systems to coordinate across horizontal organizational structures (Wheeler and Chin, 1991; Hult, 1995). A few of these elements include:

- Collective, democratic decision-making,
- Rotating tasks, functions, and roles,
- Acknowledging and legitimating the use of non-bureaucratic, nonmeritocratic considerations in hiring, advancement, and other personnel decisions, and
- Egalitarian distribution of rewards.

Hybrid feminist bureaucratic forms

Most feminist organizations have hybrid structures that combine conventional and innovative structures to balance their feminist principles with the demands of the market. One notable hybrid is the "feminist bureaucracy" (Ashcraft, 2001) characterized by fluid and negotiable relationships and ongoing tension between individual and community development. Within this hybrid, members grapple with the "organized dissonance" among the presumably contradictory elements, focusing on integrating hierarchical and egalitarian modes of power.

A second hybrid is "relational bureaucracy" (Gittell and Douglass, 2012) that brings bureaucracy's rational, role-based relationships together with structures that embed more personal and connected relationships into the roles of customers, workers, and managers. This hybrid enables the caring, specific, and knowledgeable responsiveness made possible by strong relationships with the scalability, replicability, and sustainability found in bureaucracies. And even without significant structural differences, it's possible for organizations to redirect the same structures designed for their normal work to serve additional purposes, such as when organizations intentionally work to develop compassion, caring, and empathy (Worline and Dutton, 2017).

Governance

Feminists have also experimented with forms of organizational governance, the overarching system of rules, practices, and processes by which a firm is directed and controlled (Halley et al., 2018). Governance essentially involves balancing the interests of a company's many stakeholders, such as shareholders, management, customers, suppliers, financiers, government, and the community. Feminist interventions in corporate governance have, for example, expected board members and trustees to work individually and with the organization to advocate for feminist social change (Machold, Ahmed, and Farquhar, 2008). Feminist governance relationships ask the organization to care about all of its stakeholders (Liedtka, 1996).

Employee and member ownership

When feminist organizations want members to be fully invested in the success of their organization and to participate equally in directing the firm, they often structure themselves as cooperatives. Ranging from cooperatives wholly owned by employees to corporations where employees are the majority stakeholders, feminist ownership structures let employees enjoy additional authority and participate in the financial growth of the business. This leads to greater income equality and to a fairer sharing of the financial and non-financial benefits of increased productivity and profitability. Even organizations with conventional ownership and authority structures can set up their own more democratic governance and revenue-sharing by collectively creating an organizational constitution, following the feminist practices of companies like Loomio.

Fully sustainable business models

Feminist businesses face a steep learning curve in their efforts to be commercially successful while also being socially, economically, and ecologically sustainable. Feminist businesses believe that generating profits by extracting value from all kinds of human, material, and social resources without renewing them violates feminist principles of whole humanness and generativity. They design business models for generating revenue while regenerating resources, creating new kinds of value, and demonstrating feminist values (Harquail, 2017).

Feminist alternative structures have been criticized for being idealist, ineffective, and impossible to scale to larger and more complex businesses. These alternatives can indeed be difficult to implement, in large part because we have little experience with them. But just as we've learned how to negotiate for a raise and give 360-degree feedback, we can learn how to make decisions democratically, develop mutually supportive relationships, and share revenue, to the benefit of all stakeholders.

Reconsidering organizational culture

Organizational culture offers members implicit and explicit answers to questions about why things are done the way they are, and what this means. Organizational culture is the complex set of values, assumptions, and beliefs that define the ways in which a firm conducts its business. Culture shapes how we see and understand organizational life.

Feminists raise questions about organizational culture (1) to make women's workplace experiences salient; (2) to identify collective, organizational-level phenomena, concepts, and constructs that contribute to gender inequity; and (3) to identify artifacts, values, beliefs, and basic assumptions about human beings and business that either support or conflict with feminist values. Feminists have also sought to put feminist values into practice in the workplace by building feminist organizational cultures.

Culture, like gender structure, has many layers (Schein, 2010). Observable artifacts manifest deeper assumptions. For example, a business's office space and furniture, when designed to fit only male bodies and tastes, can demonstrate that the organization's culture doesn't value women employees' physical comfort as much as men's (Hirst and Schwabenland, 2018).

Values are beliefs about what kind of behavior is desired and what goals are sought by the organization. The relationships between espoused values and enacted values, sometimes called "the talk" and "the walk", respectively, often reveal deeper truths about what's really important in an organization. For example, companies may explicitly espouse a value like meritocracy while regularly enacting a non-merit based preference for men by awarding men higher bonuses and more frequent promotions than women with equal job performance (Castilla and Benard, 2010). Unobservable basic assumptions, like the belief that hard work will be rewarded with career success, reside close to the core of organizational culture.

Feminists don't believe that the artifacts, values, assumptions, and interpretations of the men in power are all that define an organization's culture. Instead, they also look to understand how women and other marginalized people are experiencing and understanding their organizations. Consider how Kanter's (1977) landmark study, *Men and Women of the Corporation*, analyzed the experiences of both salaried and hourly waged women and men. She analyzed how the organization's culture centered around the values and needs of male employees, while she gave voice to the experiences of female workers kept on the margins of the organization's culture. Notably, Kanter also interviewed executives' wives, recognizing these women as non-waged contributors to the work and the culture of the business. By adding women's experiences to studies of organizations that were designed for and dominated by men, feminist cultural studies made these analyses more complete and more useful.

Feminist research also demonstrated how culture studies that ignored women's experiences produced scholarly constructs and managerial advice that was at best partial and at worst wrong. Consider just one construct, prototypical cultures. Deal and Kennedy's (1984) path-breaking *Corporate Cultures: The Rites and Rituals of Corporate Life* clustered business cultures into four types: work-hard, play-hard culture; tough-guy macho culture; process culture; and bet-the-company culture. Similarly, Cameron and Quinn's (1999) wellregarded Competing Values Framework identified its own quartet of cultural types: clan, adhocracy, market, and hierarchy. These typologies have been taken as definitive, objective, and generalizable and are regularly taught in business courses. Yet Maddock and Parkin's (1993) study of women's views of organizational cultures generated quite a different typology of the "gentleman's club," the "locker room," the "barrack yard," and the "smart macho" culture, types which overlap barely at all with the two more influential typologies. If organizational culture prototypes based on men's experiences are incommensurate with those based on women's experiences, what should we make of these differences? And, how much can we generalize from cultural research that fails to account explicitly for women's and marginalized groups' experiences?

While many mainstream culture researchers were emphasizing cultural consistency and strength, feminist scholars illustrated the plurality of understandings and experiences of culture, suggesting that organizational culture might be integrated, fragmented, or differentiated and very rarely uniform across levels and groups (Martin, 1992). Similarly, while popular studies of culture framed the function of culture as driving performance, feminist scholars expanded culture's relevance beyond "performance" to emphasize meaning and identity (Hatch and Schultz, 1996). Bringing in the voices of women and other marginalized members transforms what we know about "how things are done" in organizations.

Understanding the presence and persistence of gender inequality

Feminists also look to organizational culture to help understand the slow and jagged push towards gender equality. Businesses were once rife with blatant gender bias spanning from their policies to their cultural assumptions, and old-fashioned overt sexism was easy to see and call out. Once explicit, direct, and deliberately different treatment of women and men was prohibited, bias went underground, into the deep structure and the implicit assumptions of organization's cultures, where it remained hard at work sustaining gender inequality.

To evaluate contemporary and stealthier sexism, culture researchers have generated several constructs and measures to characterize and quantify the kinds of sexism that organizations sustain, including:

1. Second-generation gender bias,
2. Hostile sexism, and
3. Benevolent sexism.

1. *Second-generation gender bias.*

Even in organizations where no one intends to discriminate against women, "second-generation" forms of workplace gender bias can obstruct efforts towards gender equality (Ely, Ibarra, and Kolb, 2011). Choices as simple as expense policies that don't cover childcare costs when a manager is sent on an overnight business trip, or offering only beer and not also wine at the company happy hour can reflect second-generation bias against women. Second-generation bias is inherent and unconscious bias built into organizational practices and structures as well as into organizationally shared attitudes about women and men, so it easily neutralizes and countermands conscious efforts to reduce gender inequality. Second-generation bias explains, to some degree, why formal efforts to drive gender equality such as those outlined in Chapter 2, "Obstacles and approaches to gender equality in business," are not as powerful as they need to be, and why emphasizing policy alone might be inducing gender fatigue.

2. *Hostile and* 3. *Benevolent sexism.*

Culture researchers have identified two variations of sexism common in contemporary organizations: hostile and benevolent sexism (Glick and Fiske, 2001). Hostile sexism combines a desire for sexual dominance and control with the belief that the opposing gender is inferior. Benevolent sexism, in contrast, is a chivalrous, protective, and paternalistic attitude that affectionately idealizes women in their traditional and stereotypical roles. Because benevolently sexist attitudes appear positive, people often don't see how they harm women and all people or how these attitudes reproduce gendered inequality. When both types of sexism are found together, they're called "ambivalent sexism" to highlight the contradictory nature of feeling hostile and aggressive towards women, as well as affectionate and protective of women.

These days it's rare for a business to express or espouse hostile sexism. We are more likely to see benevolent sexism, such as organizational practices that steer women into customer service jobs because women are idealized as being interpersonally skilled. Indeed, many business initiatives to "value the feminine" qualities of women are more accurately understood as large-scale expressions of benevolent sexism. Benevolent sexism contributes to work, job, and role segregation as well as differential treatment of women and men. However benevolent it intends to be, this sexism subtly undermines perceptions of women's competence and contributions (King et al., 2012) and also reinforces perceptions of men's superiority.

Many culture measures are available now to assess elements that might enhance or impede gender equality, such as direct experience of sexism, tolerance for sexual harassment (Hulin, Fitzgerald and Drasgow, 1996), and gender inequality at work (Memon and Jena, 2017). Measures like Climate towards Diversity (Cox, 1993) help to shed light on how a business responds to people who differ from the privileged men around which most organizations are designed. (To assess conditions for constructive feminism, organizational culture studies could measure the presence and strength of feminist values and beliefs like those in Table 3.1 and look for evidence of individual and organizational flourishing).

In a business world where data is supposed to matter, cultural assessments with data (quantitative or qualitative) offer proof that sexism remains even when many in our "post-feminist" society don't see it or acknowledge it. For example, as companies have responded to feminist pressure to close their gendered wage gaps, companies have analyzed their salary data, discovered real and systemic disparities, published their findings, and set quantitative benchmarks and targets to measure progress towards wage parity. Because no two organizations are sexist in the same way or to the same degree, measures that help us understand each organization's specific culture and the attitudes, values, and behaviors that affect how formal policies are understood and enacted may help us suss out what to do differently.

Bodies in the workplace

Feminism reconsiders the role and value of the body to reclaim women's colonized body space, confront the ways female bodies have been disparaged, release women from being defined simply as bodies, and develop alternative, more appreciative, and more holistic understandings of bodies, embodiment, and sexuality (Plaskow, 2008). Recognizing the body as a site of human being, feminism connects (and refuses to bifurcate) the body and the mind, the corporeal and the conscious, to consider the whole human in the workplace.

Bodies play several different roles in the workplace. Bodies perform physical, cognitive, and emotional tasks that make products and deliver services. They are surfaces on and through which employees craft their identities, manage their emotions, and work to present their bodies "appropriately" in the workplace. Bodies are also organisms – living, breathing, physical, spiritual, and material sources of human effort. In businesses, bodily effort is focused on productive work. Outside of businesses, bodily effort produces, reproduces, and generates creativity, care for others, and life itself.

Thinking of human bodies as living organisms makes us acknowledge the demands of staying alive and flourishing physically. Feminists have identified significant oversights in how businesses attend to human bodies. Here, we'll address a very basic one: why doesn't business pay more attention to caring for and supporting female employees' physical bodies in the workplace?

Business's discomfort with body-related issues traces all the way back to sexist understandings of how human beings' value is determined by the gendering of bodies. A key move of patriarchy is to set up a split between the mind and the body. Mind/body dualism imagines that the mind and the body are distinct and conceptually separate elements of human nature. This separation implies that the mind and the body have different value, with all things related to the mind having higher status than any things related to the body. Men's male bodies are associated with the mind, while women's female bodies are associated with nature.

Bodies separated from minds are easy to dehumanize

The mind/body split has made it easier for businesses to treat human bodies as machines to deploy, tools to control, and inputs to consume. Early in the industrial revolution, a huge business challenge was how to bring human bodies together, control them, coordinate them, and get them to be as productive as possible. The physical and conceptual organization of slave labor on cotton plantations formed the foundation of scientific management's solution to these problems (Baptist, 2014). Applied to wage worker labor in factories and mines, these slave management techniques helped businesses think about workers as bodies that could be treated like interchangeable machine parts or widgets. Even today in many offices and retail establishments, employees are treated as interchangeable resources.

Feminism and other critical management perspectives (Hassard, Holliday and Willmott, 2000; Pullen and Rhoades, 2015) decry this approach to human bodies. Because wigitization fundamentally dehumanizes any person, it conflicts with the feminist value of whole humanness. This dehumanization of workers' bodies also echoes the historic treatment of women and women's bodies by patriarchy more broadly, by treating bodies as possessions and tools controlled by men, rather than by women themselves. Women's bodies were very rarely seen as bodies that represented beings who were fully human.

Bodies represent uncontrollable nature

Bodies continually remind business people and managers of that about workers which is not controllable, not predictable, and not reliable. The actual nature of bodies makes it difficult to standardize, reorganize, and rationalize work. Only some work can be performed by any sort of body, regardless of sex, race, or physical ability. The only way to widgetize bodies is to ignore anything about them that physically falls outside the norm and to disregard anything about them that goes beyond the physical.

Work, management, and business were organized around male bodies. Bodies were not a priority for managers' attention. Bodies were not thought of as "problems" until women came along, bringing with them their unruly, messy, hormone-driven animal bodies. Very simple things, like adding a second set of bathrooms that had more toilets and no urinals, not to mention adding breaks where women had enough time to use the toilets, became "problems" that businesses had to solve if they hired women employees. (Alternatively, organizations could use the strategy of Yale Medical School and Harvard Law School: both schools claimed that a lack of women's bathroom facilities made it impossible for them to admit women as students [Plaskow, 2008]).

Women's bodies are never the right fit within a business environment designed with males/men/masculinity as the norm (Wolkowitz, 2006). Consider that something as banal as the temperature setting in an office was designed to fit men's bodies, and for years men have made fun of women for complaining that the temperature was too low for women's comfort. Desks, tables, and tools were all designed to fit male bodies and not fit female ones.

It's surprising how little progress has been made towards simply creating a physical business environment that accommodates the bodily needs of women – pregnant women, postpartum women, lactating women, menopausal women, and menstruating women. Something as human and commonplace as menstruation is not normalized or accepted in the workplace. We don't see tampons and pads right next to the toilet paper in the office bathrooms. And although pregnant female bodies often need more breaks and less weight-bearing work, many companies balk at adjusting the physical work requirements of pregnant employees (Gatrell, Cooper, and Kossek, 2017). These normal functions of female bodies have little support in the workplace.

Breastfeeding bodies interfere with working bodies

Even more than pregnancy, it's breastfeeding that challenges the ways business understands employees' bodies as independent, autonomous sources of productive effort. Breastfeeding requires the ongoing, regular, intimate, physical interaction between a mother and her child, and the conventional workplace has chosen not to accommodate this. To make the mother–child breastfeeding relationship possible during work, businesses would need to permit nursing children to come into the workplace to connect with their mothers, or allow their mothers to leave work once or twice a day to go feed their babies.

The unquestioned workplace assumption that bodies are tools of work production makes it difficult to honor breastfeeding as a physical relationship between two human bodies: the mother's and the child's. Instead, business conversations about breastfeeding at work focus not on breastfeeding, but rather on milk production. Businesses that purport to accommodate breastfeeding really just make milk production a little easier, by finding women places and time for pumping and storing breast milk. Breast milk is treated as a product, produced, and bottled much like milk from a cow, for a child to consume off-premises. Reducing breastfeeding to a challenge of production and packaging translates it to something business understands. In contrast, the intimate, embodied, mother–child relationship in which breastfeeding ideally occurs is not something businesses can fathom (Lee, 2018).

Some businesses now provide lactation breaks and lactation rooms for mothers to pump their breast milk, while others offer chairs inside supply closets next to broken copy machines. Higher status employees have some discretion over their schedules and can find time for regular pumping, but hourly workers and lower status workers often don't even have time to pump, much less a clean and quiet place in which to do it. The lack of facilities for milk production or ways for infants to stay nearby demonstrates that most businesses don't fully support or intend to accommodate nursing mothers. Breastfeeding workers are asked to prioritize on-site paid work over infant feeding, even in a culture that supposedly encourages women to breastfeed for six months for healthier babies. Without making it possible for mothers to breastfeed infants while at work in the workplace during breaks in work tasks, businesses make it impossible for women to work in a business for pay and simultaneously judged to be "good" mothers. Few businesses really care to help current workers who are nursing mothers or future workers who are nursing children.

Dressing to manage women's bodies

Women's bodies at work are always available to be scrutinized, judged, and evaluated against sexist standards of appropriateness. Because women's bodies are reminders of sexuality, women at work need to cover and hide the "female" parts of their bodies to focus more on presenting "respectable business femininity" (Mavin and Grandy, 2016). Women perform extra work to meet expectations for professional dress in male-dominated cultures where they don't want to be mistaken as potential sex partners rather than business colleagues (Rafaeli et al., 1997). Women employees, especially professional women, are expected to be fit, not fat. Fitness signals professionalism. It demonstrates that the worker is in control of her body and has the energy to endure hard work. In contrast, chubbiness supposedly signals laziness, self-indulgence, and sensuousness, which are not desirable qualities in the masculine workplace. Women recognize that both men and women will evaluate their appearances and punish them if they miss the mark.

Male bodies age incrementally, and male bodies fit the linear career paths designed for men. Female bodies experience more kinds of bodily cycles for over half their adult lives, such as with pregnancy and menstruation. Even after menopause, when pregnancy is no longer possible and menstrual cramps are a fading memory, women's bodies still don't become more acceptable in the workplace. Instead, women are presumed to be compromised by hormonal imbalances, and once these pass women are simply too old (Gatrell, Cooper, and Kossek, 2017).

While male bodies remain reliable, contained, and easy to discipline to fit the workplace, female bodies can't conform. Women can't schedule their bodies' modes in advance or postpone them for a business trip. And while individual women can choose to reduce their bodies' misfit with work (e.g., choose not to bear children), that's no solution to the larger problem of workplaces designed not to fit women's bodies. Women's bodies and females' natural, predictable movements through human reproductive work continue to confront business's assumptions that bodies – especially female bodies – don't matter enough to be fully supported in the workplace.

Harmful workplace experiences

Violence is ubiquitous in the workplace. No one thinks violence is desirable in the workplace, but it certainly is normal, especially once you consider the range of organizational and employee behaviors that fit the definition of violence. Violence in the workplace is any behavior that harms the body, psyche, capability, or personhood of an employee. Violence in the workplace can be experienced and expressed through actions as dramatic as murder and physical harm, as gendered as sexual coercion, as nasty as bullying, and as prosaic as incivility.

Violence is rooted in and fostered by many assumptions about what makes a business effective. For example, the emphasis on business rationality punishes those who express emotion and the emphasis on obedience punishes those who want to demonstrate agency. Dominance and aggressive behavior are so much a part of how we define leadership and how we define the masculinity that shapes business norms that we aren't surprised when leaders' and coworkers' behaviors veer towards violence. We're not shocked when managers overrule a team's decision, laugh at employees' mistakes, or speak rudely about clients, even when we recognize that this behavior causes harm.

Feminists raise concern about violence at work, because what is defined as violent behavior, what is experienced as violence, and why violence is deployed at work are all shaped by gendered norms and reinforce inequality. Violence affects women, and men in marginal groups, differently than men in privileged groups. Women are much more likely than men to become targets of specifically gendered violence such as sexual harassment, gender-based discrimination, and negative attitudes towards women, as well as violence that doesn't seem inherently gendered, such as overwork, bullying, or incivility. The harm directed at women is especially powerful because women, as subordinates both organizationally and culturally, have fewer options for defending themselves against violence (Salin, 2003). On average, women are more emotionally vulnerable, physically smaller, and more concentrated in precarious work, low-status work, and customer service roles that leave women with little organizational protection or security.

Feminists like Frances Perkins, who designed the Fair Labor Standards Act that limited laborers' formal work week to 40 hours, have always advocated to protect women and all people from being abused, injured, or violated at work or by work. Feminists have pioneered efforts:

• To understand, name, respond to, and prevent the specific problem of men's violence against women inside and outside the workplace,

- To establish legal and social protections for the victims of men's violence,
- To include domestic violence and handgun control as workplace issues,
- To criminalize some violent behavior and make other kinds of violence socially unacceptable at work, and
- To undermine cultural and institutional supports for violence against women and all people in the workplace and beyond.

This work has included identifying constructs like sexual harassment that make gendered violence visible (Farley, 1978; MacKinnon, 1978), investigating gendered and nongender-specific violent behaviors, and proposing ways to change the interpersonal, cultural, and structural conditions in the workplace that support this violence. Feminists recognize that every form of violence at work interferes with our collective ability to flourish as individuals, as communities, and as businesses.

Violence creates and sustains domination and oppression

Violence is central to oppression, to domination, and to the experience of being subordinated. Dominance is the defining feature of patriarchal systems, and violence is the policing apparatus of patriarchy. Men's violence, masculine violence, and patriarchal attitudes about violence work to perpetuate men's power over women and some men's power over other men. More broadly, all systems of oppression, not only sexism but also racism, heterosexism, capitalism, and the kyriarchy as a whole rely on violence or threat of violence to sustain the domination of one group over others (Collins, 2017). What is power-over, if not a threat of violence?

Wherever we see gendered inequality in the workplace, we know that violence and the threat of violence are being used to sustain women's and men's subordination. However, gendered violence against women is intended not simply to direct, control, and dominate women, but also – specifically – to punish women who dare to think, act, or expect to be treated as equals to men (Beard, 2017). It's a form of patriarchal law enforcement. Sexual harassment, in particular, is a way that men claim the workplace as masculine turf, to make women feel different and less valued, and to ensure that women never feel completely at ease (Schultz, 1998).

Violence supports obedience

Organizations depend on the ability of a few to control and coordinate the behaviors of many. We imagine that control and coordination are achieved through power that feels entirely legitimate, such as the authority of a skilled engineer over a newbie engineer. At the same time, we know that a significant portion of obedience in organizations comes from forms of authority that are less legitimate – or not legitimate at all – and that business wrongly assumes it has put outside its magic circle. Members of dominant social groups will too often use the relative status, social authority, and power that goes along with their social positions to augment or supersede their formal positions of authority in a business and help them sustain the status quo of social inequality.

Consider a recent study documenting that women are more likely than men to experience bullying at work. While men were typically bullied by supervisors who had formal power over them, women were bullied by both superiors and peers. Further, while none of the male victims reported being bullied by subordinates, one-fifth of the women reported being bullied by people below them in the organizational hierarchy (Salin, 2003). Peer and subordinate bullies didn't feel constrained by having equal or less formal power than their women targets.

Sexual harassment

While expressions of sexuality per se are not necessarily discriminatory or oppressive (Hearn et al., 1989; Williams, Guiffre, and Dellinger, 1999), sexual harassment is a clearly gendered, sexualized form of violence. In the workplace, an experience is considered sexualized violence if it inappropriately imposes sexuality on individuals. For example, sexualized experiences are actions that draw attention to aspects of an individual's sexual life, value individuals exclusively for their sexual appeal, or, in general, treat individuals as objects available for sexual use (Sojo, Wood, and Genat, 2016). All unwanted sexualized behaviors that threaten a person's physical and emotional well-being can be understood as sexual harassment.

The common understanding of sexual harassment is that it involves predatory efforts to force sexual contact and otherwise coerce the victim physically (e.g., rape). However, less invasive forms of violence are also sexual harassment, including patronizing behavior that is sexist but not overtly sexualized, and taunting behavior such as sexual gestures, physical displays, and personal comments that create a sexualized hostile environment (Chamberlain et al., 2008).

Sexual harassment is pervasive and frequent. A comprehensive study of workplace harassment in the United States concluded that "anywhere from 25% to 85% of women report having experienced sexual harassment in the workplace" (U.S. Equal Employment Opportunity Commission, 2016, p. 8). It's a wide range, but even at its most conservative estimate, the amount of harassment is overwhelming. Men were predominantly responsible for sexual harassment against women in the workplace, but smaller numbers of men were targets and some perpetrators were women.

Sexual harassment is commonly assumed to be about sex, a problem of misunderstood mating behavior. Thinking of sexual harassment as the result of biological urges, as though it's simply "testosterone on overdrive," is a strategy for making sexual harassment seem normal. As feminists have helped business and society understand, sexual harassment is not about sex, but about illegitimate power. It is a profound form of sexualized, gendered violence in the workplace.

Incivility and micro-aggressions

Incivility, on the other hand, looks like it does no real harm. Enacted through behaviors like disrespect and condescension, incivility is low-intensity behavior with ambiguous intent to harm the target, that violates workplace norms for mutual respect (Andersson and Pearson, 1999). With incivility, victims are hurt first by the action, and again by its ambiguous intent. That a victim has to question whether the incivility was deliberate helps the harm burrow deeper.

Incivility is not quite as dramatic as sexual harassment. It makes no physical threat and expects no obedient response. It doesn't seem to be driven by organizational position. And, it's relatively normalized. People are unpleasant, condescending, and sharp with each other so often that it's not terribly shocking. As a form of workplace violence, incivility doesn't even seem to be gender-related. However, women, along with men of color, are more often targeted by incivility than are White men.

This "selective incivility" towards men of color and women is the veiled manifestation of sexism and racism in organizations (Cortina et al., 2013; Sherman, 2015). Because the intent behind perpetrators' efforts to harm the target is ambiguous, perpetrators can plausibly deny to themselves and others that they intended harm or that their actions were driven by bias. Selective incivilities are much like micro-aggressions (Pierce et al., 1978). Micro-aggressions are "brief and commonplace daily verbal, behavioral, and environmental indignities, whether intentional or unintentional, that communicate hostile, derogatory, or negative slights and insults towards members" of oppressed groups (Nadal, 2008, p. 23). Perpetrators are often unaware that their own implicit bias is driving them to treat others in biased, harmful ways.

Not many colleagues and companies recognize the harm caused by sexist jokes, sexist language, selective incivility, and micro-aggression. Yet, these lower intensity, pervasive, and frequent hurtful experiences damage individual women and people and sustain a sexist environment (Cortina et al., 2013). Immediately and over time, this harm reduces women's work performance, as well as their sense of autonomy, safety, and belongingness.

Sexual harassment, selective incivility, and micro-aggressions, like all other forms of gendered violence in organizations, work to degrade, offend, and intimidate individual women and women as a group. This violence diminishes women's performance and wellbeing at work (Sojo, Wood, and Genat, 2016). Frequent, lower intensity violence like incivility is just as effective at harming women at work as less frequent, higher intensity violence like sexual harassment. Both are harmful expressions of sexism.

Businesses need to recognize the full range of gendered abusive behaviors as violence directed towards women and intended to reinforce gender inequality. Businesses need to protect all employees from workplace violence by changing organizational norms as well as perpetrators' behavior. Only then can businesses begin to craft organizations where all people feel safe, secure, and encouraged to bloom.

Models of leadership and expressions of power

As a topic, a quality, and a practice, leadership has pride of place in the business world. Leadership is promoted both as the critical solution for problems and as the critical tool for individual and business advancement. It's through leadership that individuals and companies win at the game of business.

Because leadership is glamorized as such a potent force, it is a popular topic in business press and business education. Harvard Business School offers nearly a dozen different leadership courses for executives alone. Focusing on leadership lends prestige to business programs, teaching, and research.

Feminists, however, have long been suspicious of "leadership" and the primacy that businesses place on it. Traditional treatments of leadership have been closely associated with hierarchy and positional power, and thus inextricably linked with the patriarchal domination of women.

Feminists also don't like the ways that leadership research and practice have lionized the achievements of solo individuals (Sinclair, 2014) as superhero action figures in organizationally privileged positions with their superior status reinforced by their gender (male), race (white), and class (upper-middle and ascendant). Feminists do not believe that this kind of leadership permits either equality or flourishing, even if it can deliver financial business results.

Leadership is a way of exerting power (see Box 3.2 for a discussion of different expressions of power). Leadership models, then, are theories and practices of wielding power in ways that are presented as organizationally, socially, and financially legitimate. Leadership is power that has been sanctioned, power that is celebrated, power that is assumed to be positive for everyone involved. Leadership and the power it represents are a privilege bestowed more often upon white men than on people of any other group. Thus, both legitimated dominance over others and elite white male privilege are reproduced by the ways we think about and practice leadership.

Many believe that if we could get more women into leadership positions, the problems of gender inequality would get solved. At the very least, more women in leadership would prove (as if proof were needed) that a woman could contribute as much to a business as a man. For some, the solution would be simple parity, with women and men in proportionally equal numbers of leadership positions. Others would go further, and expect (or hope) that as women achieved positions of power, they would use this power to help other women rise and also to help women as a group by changing the structures, policies, and cultures of businesses.

However, feminist investigations into conventional leadership models and feminist research in organizations have helped us see how far-fetched these expectations are, given the sustained, routine, and systemized way that women are discriminated against as potential leaders. We have learned, for example, that it's harder for women than men to achieve leadership positions. Women's positions often differ from men's in their quality and implicit importance, and women are evaluated against higher standards than men for leadership excellence and receive more severe punishments for any leadership errors (Elsesser and Lever, 2011).

Traditional patriarchal leadership

Leadership models are microcosms of gendered, raced, and classed power dynamics. The traditional model against which all others are compared is the patriarchal model, where the definition of good leadership is composed of stereotypically masculine traits. Good leaders demonstrate autonomy, control, assertiveness, domination, authority, and rationality. This heroic individual leader is a man, of course. He is also a decision-maker, a man who provides the vision, mission, and goals for his organization. He inspires motivation (or compliance) in others and he directs their behaviors. Patriarchal leadership is also paternalistic, because this leader makes decisions on behalf of followers who are supposedly unable to decide for themselves.

Patriarchal leadership, by rooting itself in the gendered binary, implicitly presents femininity (and by extension, females and women) as "not leaders" – the opposite of leaders. Women aren't masculine, and if leaders are masculine, then women are not leaders. This model quietly legitimates the expectation that male leaders should have authority over women, even when women and men hold the same jobs.

Unexamined assumptions skew our understanding of leadership

In business, we're not talking about "leadership" per se, but rather leadership in a business already well-controlled and coordinated by owners and owners' interests. Businesses specifically enable the forms of influence that have been defined as leadership. Business leaders often have many organizational tools at hand with which to threaten, intimidate, pressure, and "motivate" their followers. For example, business leaders can punish those who fail to follow their lead by giving them poor performance appraisals, by denying them pay increases, and by firing them. These are not tools that leaders in general have available to wield.

Business leadership is also anchored to the organizational structure in which it's being deployed. The opportunity to exert leadership or be seen as a leader is still tied to one's position in an organization, such that the VP of Manufacturing is "the" leader of the manufacturing department by virtue of his place in their hierarchy, rather than because he inspires others. Similarly, we'd never expect a worker in the warehouse to lead a business, no matter how important it might be to fill orders on time.

Leading itself is often assumed to be a good way to manage people, although leading and managing are not the same skills. Conflating management and leadership means that business limits leadership situations to business-related challenges. For example, businesses want to maintain order, follow established procedures, and pursue goals that the owners and top managers have chosen undemocratically. Consider that the skills needed to lead subordinates to pursue the goals of owners and top managers are different from those needed to lead a community to challenge police brutality.

Because business seems to believe that leadership is a generalized skill applicable to any context, models of leadership have largely ignored contexts outside the male-dominated domains of business, war, and sports. This means we have missed the leadership challenges, practices, and role models that can be found in public administration (with leaders like Frances Perkins), social movements (with leaders like Ella Baker and Fannie Lou Hammer), social work (with leaders like Jane Addams), and education (with leaders like Paulo Friere).

Still, even though the qualities of the followers, the qualities of the organizational structure, the challenges to be faced, and the resources at hand all work to enable and shape "leadership," business still treats leadership as a personal quality that an individual can learn and deploy wherever he goes.

Evolution of leadership models

On the surface, leadership theorizing has been very adaptive to social and technological changes. As soon as a powerful criticism begins to be mobilized, we see the leadership conversation evolve. Three updates to patriarchal leadership include:

1. *Enlightened leadership* models, with revised understandings of masculinity,
2. *Women in (male) leadership*, with women trying to perform leadership as much like men as possible, and
3. *Feminine leadership*, with women wielding femininity and feminine power.

1. Enlightened leadership models.
Enlightened leadership is my term for a group of leadership models that take as their subject a person (still mostly masculine) who has a more enlightened, updated, modern understanding of his paternal role (imagine switching channels from *Mad Men* to *The Office*). These models include (and aren't limited to)

"post heroic leadership" (Fletcher, 2003), authentic leadership, transformational leadership, servant leadership, stewardship, and distributed leadership. These models all present themselves as distinct from and in contrast to the traditional patriarchal model. They also appear to be more welcoming to women than the traditional model, but that's an illusion.

As a group, these enlightened leadership models shift emphasis away from competition, hierarchy, task orientation, instrumentality, transactions, and outcomes, and towards collaboration, lateral connections, process orientation, relationships, consent, and follower engagement and participation. They suggest something more like shared or distributed leadership, and often concern themselves with meeting followers' needs.

Because the traditional connection between these behaviors and femininity and submissiveness can unconsciously make these behaviors unattractive to both leaders and followers, enlightened leadership is often adopted only superficially (Fletcher, 2003). Instead of challenging the notion of power-over, the transformational leader remains styled as a great man (or woman), subtly but surely relying on the hierarchical structure and the common knowledge of who is in charge and who is a follower ultimately to get things done. This fellow is still a hero, but he's humbler. He leads quietly and often credits his colleagues and subordinates for their contributions, but still enjoys the power of his hierarchical role among with the notion that he did it, if not individually, by having something "more" than the rest – by having been the leader. Behind the soft touch, enlightened leadership is still power-over.

Box 3.2 EXPRESSIONS OF POWER

Leadership is fundamentally about power – holding it, exercising it, changing the distribution and relations of power, and being conscious of one's own power. The typology of expressions of power following starts with Follett's (1924) distinction between power-over and power-with, and has since been expanded by practitioners (especially Batliwala, 2011).

Power can manifest in both negative and positive forms, ranging from domination and resistance to collaboration and transformation. Three positive expressions of power challenge us to see the best in each other and help each other contribute, grow, and succeed, while the two negative expressions of power pit people against one another.

Positive expressions of power

Power-to is agency, a person's individual ability to act. It is rooted in the belief that every individual has the "power to" make a difference by acknowledging her own sources of power and by acting on them, especially in ways that allow others to access their own sources of power.

Power-with is collective action, when a person or group uses their sources of power to share resources and decision-making, or to work with each other so that the collective makes its own decisions.

Power-within refers to the inner qualities that a person or group has or can develop to overcome obstacles and fear, to step forward with ideas, and to take action for change. It includes intangible resources such as knowledge, EQ, access to information, influence, contacts, and other valuable personal resources.

Negative expressions of power

Power-over is oppressive power used to direct, control, dominate, exploit, take advantage of and/or make decisions for others, as well as to control valuable resources (time, money, energy, water, etc.) (Power-over is distinct from authority granted democratically to an agent or institution).

Power-under is the destructive power of sabotage and subversion, which can be released along with constructive energy when people get good and angry about being powerless. Their anger fuels both efforts to dominate others and efforts to change the system.

All models of leadership build on power-to. Conventional leadership models rely on power-over, while feminist leadership practices rely on positive expressions of power-with, power-to, and power-within.

The transformational potential of enlightened leadership models gets coopted – "bropropriated" again – because although these models of leadership should be rooted in a view of power that is more interdependent and egalitarian, people privileged by patriarchal models often don't want to change. It's too risky to swap a proven method with a genuinely enlightened one. They have too much privilege and power-over to lose. So while leaders might present themselves as enlightened, they are ready to fall back on conventional leadership if their authority is challenged.

For women, it's also risky to adopt enlightened leadership behaviors, but for different reasons. These enlightened models seem to encourage the very behaviors women might prefer, yet women find these behaviors difficult to use successfully because they can't get other people to recognize their feminine behaviors as leadership efforts. Empowerment and collaboration require mutuality, reciprocity, and giving back some ideas, as well as receiving them. But when women contribute, or listen, or help, people often interpret these behaviors as gifts and don't feel they need to reciprocate or respond with the effort that shared leadership requires (Fletcher, 2003). Thus, for women as well as men, the promise of enlightened leadership is often diminished.

2. Women in (male) leadership: women imitating men.

A second stream of leadership practice has looked for ways to fit women into patriarchal models of leadership, largely by teaching potential leaders who are women how to be more like leaders who are men. The desire to fit women into (male) leadership models coordinates nicely with gender equality approaches of "add women and stir," "fix the women," "GirlBoss," and "up the ladder, ladies!" It focuses on adjusting, teaching, and encouraging women to display more masculine leadership characteristics, to be more heroic, more assertive, and more leaderly. Women can learn how to play men's games with men's rules (Heim, 1992). And, once women act like men, women's leadership will be recognized. Of course, fitting themselves into a traditional, paternalistic image of a leader requires women to suppress other qualities, particularly ones that seem too feminine. The women in (male) leadership model makes it hard for women leaders to be authentic (Ely, Ibarra, and Kolb, 2011).

The idea that women and men have different leadership abilities, styles, and behaviors is poorly supported by data (Klenke, 2011). It seems that our stereotypes and gendered expectations are so strong that we believe that these differences exist, and also that they matter. Where data does demonstrate differences is when people *evaluate* male and female leaders. For example, people are more likely to evaluate women negatively when women exhibit a masculine leadership style than when women exercise leadership in a more stereotypical feminine way (Eagly, Makhijani, and Klonsky, 1992). Negative evaluations of women leaders are stronger when women occupy male-dominated roles, and when the evaluators are male themselves.

One explanation for gender bias in evaluating women leaders is "role congruity" – the ways that men and women leaders' behaviors fit or do not fit with socially stereotypical expectations for these genders. For example, women leaders who demonstrate nurturing behavior or attention to relationships fit social stereotypes for women's roles better than women leaders who are unemotional, directive, or aggressive (Eagly and Karau, 2002).

Bias in people's evaluations of women leaders often occurs when they evaluate women leaders against two standards simultaneously:

1. A feminine stereotype of how "women" are supposed to behave, and
2. A masculine stereotype about how "leaders" should behave.

These conflicting standards put women leaders in a double bind, where neither choice of behavior satisfies both expectations at once and thus choices are bad ones.

In addition, White women leaders and women leaders of color may also be evaluated against negative stereotypes of powerful women that threaten to emasculate men. White women might face the stereotype of a nagging mother, while Black women might face the stereotype of the angry matriarch (Jean-Marie,

Williams, and Sherman, 2009). Conflicting stereotypes lead people to perceive women as competent or liked, but rarely both; Exhibit A: Hillary Clinton. Essentially, no matter how women leaders act, they are in danger of upsetting some observer or colleague's gendered expectations for how women who are leaders should behave.

False hopes raised by women in (male) leadership

Programs focusing on getting women to adopt traditionally male leadership styles as well as a few leadership programs that include opportunities for women to consider enlightened models and feminine models of leadership have helped some women to move up in business's hierarchies (Ely, Ibarra, and Kolb, 2011). Yet, fitting women into (male) leadership may also have raised individual women's hopes, leading them to expect that changing their behavior will convince others to evaluate their contributions fairly relative to men, and leading other women to expect women leaders to advance gender equality in their businesses. The irony is that by the time women have adapted and accommodated to male-standard expectations of leaders, many have lost not only their ability to act differently (e.g., more like "women"), but also lost their ability to offer transformative perspectives.

3. *Feminine leadership.*
A different way of getting women into leadership roles is to encourage them to be more feminine in how they lead. Building on gender equality approaches to "value the feminine" and skirting close to benevolent sexism, businesses have suggested that women adopt an explicitly feminine model of leadership. Women are to commit further to demonstrating empathy, listening skills, vulnerability, concern for relationships, nurturing, and collaboration skills. This approach has the added benefit, many argue, of allowing women to be authentic.

Some researchers propose feminine leadership models as leadership-specific "gateway feminist" approaches to gender equality. For example, "connective leadership" (LipmanBlumen, 1992), networking, sharing responsibility, interlinking with each other's goals, considering things contextually and as systems rather than isolated pieces, prioritizing responsiveness, and other features that would create a "web of inclusion and care" (Helgesen, 1995) would allow women to contribute to businesses in ways newly recognized as leadership. Perhaps, even, women leaders who were already succeeding were doing so precisely because they were using feminine behaviors, the very behaviors previously thought to be inappropriate to leaders (Rosener, 1990).

Feminine expressions of power
The feminine leadership model assumes that being female/feminine requires a different orientation to power, one that is less self-focused and individualistic,

and instead more relational. This orientation looks like power-with. It's possible that power-with fits well with femininity. It's also possible that power-with is learned when people collaborate with each other to achieve these goals in spite of the formal or informal (male) power structure. What are marked as "feminine" influence techniques may simply be those used by women who've learned how to navigate as powerless subordinates. Strangely enough, women may have learned these skills and learned to appreciate them from having been kept outside the structure of conventional power in the first place (Baker-Miller, 1976).

On the positive side, feminine leadership models challenge the dominant idea that leadership must be conventionally masculine. However, there are many problems with feminine leadership models. Three that stand out include:

- These models are implicitly racist. The research and theorizing on which they were built failed to include the experiences of Black women and other women of color (Parker, 2006), and thus don't reflect how women of color define femininity or leadership.
- Feminine leadership gives the misleading impression that women actually do lead through stereotypically feminine behaviors and that women are different from men in significant ways, when the data does not support this (Billing and Alvesson, 2000).
- Feminine leadership reinforces a gendered division of (leadership) labor, creating the possibility that women may be exploited for their special skills (Billing and Alvesson, 2000).

Feminine leadership has helped to raise the profile of additional enlightened leadership behaviors, helped some women claim leadership skills that feel authentic to them, and perhaps made room to appreciate the efforts of men who use feminine skills to lead. However, feminine leadership models fail to challenge the gendered power structure or the basic goals and values of conventional businesses (Calas and Smircich, 1993) and thus cannot advance full gender equality or serve a transformational agenda.

What about *feminist* leadership?

Feminists don't want women to pretend to be patriarchs, to develop trusting relationships with people they keep subordinated, or to demonstrate any kind of heroism. Feminists want people to lead differently by demonstrating and advocating feminist values and pursuing social justice.

Consider this working definition of feminist leadership, drawn from the work of global social justice advocate Srilatha Batliwata (2011, p. 29). Feminist leadership is:

> [women and people] with a feminist perspective and vision of social justice, individually and collectively transforming themselves to use their power, resources,

and skills in non-oppressive, inclusive structures and processes to mobilize others – especially other women (and marginalized men) – around a shared agenda of social cultural economic and political transformations for equality [and flourishing for all].

Now imagine this leadership directed towards the social and business goals of a company. What might this feminist leadership practice create in a business, that other leadership models would miss?

Feminist leadership practices differ from conventional, enlightened, and feminine leadership models in critical ways, including:

1. *Feminist leadership is a practice more than it is an abstract theoretical or academic model.*
Unlike with other models of leadership, there are no best-selling leadership books and relatively few management articles promoting feminist leadership practice (exceptions include Follett, 1924; Barton, 2006; Sinclair, 2014). Instead, feminist leadership is discussed in feminist organizations' handbooks and histories (Koen, 1984), social movement manuals (Just Associates, 2016), and NGO white papers (Batliwala, 2011). My analysis, following, draws heavily on these practical resources, as well as academic sources.

Feminist leadership appears mostly in practical handbooks for organization members on the ground, not just because it challenges the status quo of management so profoundly, but also because it is an actively evolving set of practices that does not pretend to offer generic "how to" advice. Instead, feminist leadership practice asks contributors to focus on ways they can address their specific organizational challenges, with the resources they have at hand and with the people who are present, to put feminist principles and values into action. Practices emerge as contributors experiment with different ways to resolve the tensions between principles, diverse experiences, and local conditions and opportunities (Brown, 1992).

2. *Feminist leadership practice is co-created, shared, and the property of a group.*
Feminist leadership practice establishes a very different relationship between the people doing the leading and the people being led. For feminist leadership, these are the same people. There are no "followers," only co-leaders.

I use the term co-leaders to emphasize that feminist practices ask contributors to participate as peers, equal in status and value. (The more common term "shared leadership" isn't precise about the status and power differences or similarities among group members. "Shared" doesn't mean that followers participate as equals to leaders. It just means that they have some leadership role to play along with their followership role). Even when some members have more formal status or higher organizational roles, feminist leadership practices rely on peer-to-peer interaction. Interacting with other group members as peers helps groups avoid the ways that formal or informal authority or status differences might change how any participant's contributions are treated, to ensure that all valuable contributions can be recognized.

3. *Feminist leadership practices are designed around power-with.*
Mary Parker Follett (1924), the first management theorist to discuss collective power, coined the phrases "power-over" and "power-with" to help highlight the dynamics of control and dominance present in traditional discussions of ideas about leadership in management. Follett did not believe power-over could be eliminated. Instead, she asked organizations to wean themselves from their reliance on power-over. One way to do this is to disconnect models of effective leadership from power-over, and instead to create more power-with.

Feminist leadership seeks to redistribute power and responsibilities through peer-to-peer consultation, participation, and consensus-building. A contributor's ability to influence others comes not from their positional power, but from the quality of their relationships, their interpersonal skills, and their expertise. In addition, they earn authority by using their formal status and positional authority carefully, sparingly, and lightly, by sharing their power with others, and by acting inclusively.

Networks of peer relationships stretch laterally across stakeholder groups inside and outside them, rather than up and down like ladders or pyramids based on power-over. Co-leading and group decision-making processes pool together the strengths of all participants, including not only their technical expertise, their knowledge, and their experiences, but also their relational skills, their ability to listen, and their emotional energy. When leadership is detached from an image of a solo individual doing all the leading for themselves and others, it's easier to see leadership as an emergent property of a collective of people working together.

4. *Feminist leadership practices have a transformative agenda.*
Unlike other models of leadership which imagine leadership deployed to achieve results for the business alone, feminist leadership practice has a transformative agenda where the business supports the flourishing of everyone, from the individual participant to the planet.

• *Transforming each individual participant:*
  Feminist leadership practices encourage each individual to reflect on their participation, introspect into their motivations, and constructively criticize their individual contributions as well as the workings of the group. Co-leaders learn to see themselves as accountable to each other, to their organizations, and to their business objectives, as well as to a larger social movement for equality, justice, and flourishing.
• *Transforming all participants:*
  Feminist leadership seeks to teach participants how to understand, claim, develop, and contribute their leadership skills, so that every woman, man,

and person in the network builds leadership capacity and vision. It also helps people address their roles in sustaining and changing gendered inequality and privilege.

- *Transforming the organization or business as a whole:*
Feminist leadership practices constantly challenge, experiment with, and rethink organizational policies, norms, structure, and culture. They envision organizations that achieve equality, expand diversity, and support flourishing.

- *Transforming the world outside the business:*
Even in businesses, feminist leadership practices engage participants in macro issues outside the business's boundaries, such as the community, the local environment, the political environment, and even world peace and a healthy planet. This attention to such global and even distant concerns is risible to some, who imagine it is idealistic or even ridiculous for a business team to care about world peace. Consider, though, the number of social enterprises that address one or more of these larger concerns. And, think how considering these issues while making business decisions might help a company change its business for the better. For example, thinking more globally has led some companies to phase out the use of conflict minerals, child labor, or electricity generated from burning coal, while others now serve only vegetarian meals in their lunchrooms.

- *Transforming gender structure to achieve social justice:*
Feminist leadership practice explicitly addresses gendered power dynamics and social justice, locally and immediately in group interactions as well as broadly in a business's organizational structure, client relationships, and industry/community contributions.

5. Feminist leadership is experimental, affirmative, and prefigurative.
Feminist leadership practices continually negotiate the relationship between values, actions, and specific situations. Leadership is driven as much by the situation and needs of the work at hand as it is by the abstract values it seeks to demonstrate (Follett, 1924). Because of this ongoing negotiation, individual practices vary from situation to situation and are often experimental.

Experimentation is required because feminists believe that the means by which feminists push for equality – and business results – must anticipate the end goals of equality and flourishing. For example, feminist leadership emphasizes mutually supportive relationships, healthy work habits, and joy, while avoiding as much as possible the temptation to reproduce behaviors, values, and systems that members oppose, such as dominance, wastefulness, or an extractive attitude. In this way, feminist leadership practice is "prefigurative" (Boggs, 1977), meaning that it tries to model the envisioned end situation in the ways it pursues goals.

When there are many goals and when the best paths are not clear, prefigurative experimentation is a great strategy for generating options and new practices

(Brown, 2017). Feminist leadership practices help a group use a vague and positive vision of the future to let new practices emerge, "building the bridge as they walk on it."

6. Feminist leadership makes invisible work visible, to make power visible.
Feminist leadership practices strive to make elements of leadership more transparent, so that decisions are clearly seen, vetted, and approved of by all participants. Feminist leadership practices challenge visible, hidden, and invisible power sources (such as social status), especially when these hidden sources reinforce subordination. They also work to highlight the emotional work and relational work of connection-building, empathy, listening, and accommodating that other models strive to disappear.

Feminist leadership practices can be challenging to use consistently. Emphasizing full participation, discussion, and integrative solutions takes more time than simply executing a boss's orders. The slower pace of decision-making can seem to create short-term losses. However, feminists believe that careful and caring processes, while sometimes slower, bring with them deeper understanding and commitment that result in longer-term gains.

Feminist leadership models can be difficult to enact in conventional organizations and even in transitional, "enlightened" ones. Feminists understand how easy it can be to fall back on traditional practices, especially when group members have different amounts of experience or come from several different cultures. They are always alert for hidden dynamics of hierarchy and invisible privilege. Despite and because of these difficulties, feminist leadership is creative and generative.

To get a sense of how these different models of leadership compare with each other, imagine a dinner where team members and their leader are seated together at a rectangular table:

- *Traditional patriarchal leadership* puts the man/father in an oversized chair at the head of the table, with everyone else paying attention to his cues.
- *Enlightened leadership* puts a man/father at the head of the table, pretending he's not that different from anyone else, except that people speak only when he asks them questions.
- *Women in (male) leadership* puts a woman at the head of the table in the oversized chair where the man/dad used to sit, and asks her to act just like a father, only to judge her when her outstretched arm can't reach the plate, or when she looks uncomfortable because the chair doesn't fit her.
- *Feminine leadership* puts a woman at what she's told is the head of the table, but everyone knows is actually the foot of the table, with a chair at the head ready for a man to sit in it.
- *Feminist leadership* would replace the rectangular table with a round one, with everyone in chairs of the same size, so that everyone speaks and listens to each other.

Which of these arrangements would bring out the best of each participant and make the most of the whole group?

CONCLUSION

As this chapter reimagines what business might be if feminism's concerns were addressed, several shared themes emerged:

1. For each business topic, there's an important feminist critique drawn from protective feminism, and there's an invitation to reimagine the topic in a constructive way by considering how to apply feminist business values.
2. Despite good intentions and effort, most responses to feminist critiques have been hesitant, superficial, or both. Businesses seem unwilling or unable to examine the ways their core assumptions about key elements of business depend on gendered inequality.
3. Even the most forward and "progressive" business initiatives in any of these domains (such as parental leave, or employee ownership) regularly fail to consider gender justice, a response to difference and inequality that goes beyond sameness of treatment. None of these forward-looking initiatives can resolve the problems they are intended to address; none can be as transformational as their advocates hope if business is unwilling to take steps towards transforming dynamics based on power-over and inequality into relationships reflecting justice, equality, and power-with.

Looking at these sections as a group, you can begin to see what a feminist workplace might look like – with all work treated as valuable, with our economy centered on providing for care and life, with work as a way to support flourishing, with workers and occupations valued for their contributions and not their gendering, where organizations are structured around participants as peers coordinating with democratic processes and sharing in the profits of their labor, in cultures free of discrimination where bodies (and minds, and hearts) are supported and protected from harm, and where leadership and power draw on every member's gifts, concerns, and contributions. Compared to what we get with conventional business values, this vision of a feminist alternative should be inspiring.

Even if the vision presented in these short sections seems piecemeal, incomplete, vague, or utopian, it should offer enough of a taste of what could be to entice more future-focused business people to learn about feminism, just as you have done. Share these visions with others by bringing feminist ideas more fully into your own business conversations. Perhaps you'll even consider joining with other advocates of feminist business practice to build a new kind of business, business that generates value and flourishing for everyone.

QUESTIONS

1. Table 3.1 contrasts the ways that conventional and feminist perspectives answer three questions about how business could be. What do you think the goals of business should be? What principles should businesses rely on to coordinate work and workers? What values do you think lead to business success?

2. Which of these topic sections raised issues you've not heard of before?

3. What business topic do you wish you'd seen in this chapter? How might you critique this topic, by bringing in women's voices and experiences, asking how the topic addresses gender equality, and considering what needs to change about it to support flourishing?

REFERENCES

Acker, J., 2004. 'Gender, Capitalism and Globalization'. *Critical Sociology*, 30(1), pp. 17–41.

Alchon, G., 1991. 'Mary Van Kleeck and Social-Economic Planning'. *Journal of Policy History*, 3(1), pp. 1–23.

Alvesson, M. and Billing, Y.D., 2002. 'Beyond Body-Counting: A Discussion of the Social Construction of Gender at Work'. In: I. Aaltio and A.J. Mills, eds, *Gender, Identity, and the Culture of Organizations*, London, Routledge, pp. 72–91.

Alvesson, M. and Thompson, P., 2006. 'Post-Bureaucracy?' In: S. Ackroyd, R. Batt, P. Thompson and P.S. Tolbert, ed., *The Oxford Handbook of Work and Organization*, Oxford, UK, Oxford University Press, pp. 485–507.

Anderson, E., 2017. *Private Government: How Employers Rule Our Lives (and Why We Don't Talk about It)*, Princeton, NJ, Princeton University Press.

Andersson, L.M. and Pearson, C.M., 1999, 'Tit for Tat? The Spiraling Effect of Incivility in the Workplace'. *Academy of Management Review*, 24(3), pp. 452–471.

Ashcraft, K., 2001. 'Organized Dissonance: Feminist Bureaucracy as Hybrid Form'. *Academy of Management Journal*, 44(6), pp. 1301–1322.

Baker-Miller, J., 1976. *Toward a New Psychology of Women*, Boston, MA, Beacon Press.

Baptist, E.E., 2014. *The Half Has Never Been Told: Slavery and the Making of American Capitalism*, New York, Basic Books.

Barbulescu, R. and Bidwell, M., 2013. 'Do Women Choose Different Jobs from Men? Mechanisms of Application Segregation in the Market for Managerial Workers'. *Organization Science*, 24(3), pp. 737–756.

Barton, T.R., 2006. 'Feminist Leadership: Building Nurturing Academic Communities'. *Advancing Women in Leadership Online Journal*, 21. DOI: 10.18738/awl.v20i0.250.

Batliwala, S., 2011. *Feminist Leadership for Social Transformation: Clearing the Conceptual Cloud*, New Delhi, Creating Resources for Empowerment in Action.

Beard, M., 2017. *Women & Power: A Manifesto*, New York, Liveright Publishers.

Billing, Y.D. and Alvesson, M., 2000. 'Questioning the Notion of Feminine Leadership: A Critical Perspective on the Gender Labelling of Leadership'. *Gender, Work and Organization*, 7(3), pp. 144–157.

Blau, F.D. and Kahn, L.M., 2007. 'The Gender Pay Gap: Have Women Gone as Far as They Can?'. *Academy of Management Perspectives*, 21(1), pp. 7–23.

Brown, A. M. 2017. *Emergent Strategy: Shaping Change, Shaping Worlds*. Chico, CA, AK Press.

Boggs, C., 1977. 'Marxism, Prefigurative Communism, and the Problem of Workers' Control'. *Radical America*, 6(Winter), pp. 99–122.

Bowles, H.R., Babcock, L., and Lai, L., 2007. 'Social Incentives for Gender Differences in the Propensity to Initiate Negotiations: Sometimes It Does Hurt to Ask'. *Organizational Behavior and Human Decision Processes*, 103(1), pp. 84–103.

Brescoll, V.L. and Uhlmann, E.L., 2008. 'Can an Angry Woman Get Ahead? Status Conferral, Gender, and Expression of Emotion in the Workplace'. *Psychological Science*, 19(3), pp. 268–275.

Briscoe, F. and Joshi, A., 2017. 'Bringing the Boss's Politics in: Supervisor Political Ideology and the Gender Gap in Earnings'. *Academy of Management Journal*, 60(4), pp. 1415–1441.

Brown, H., 1992. *Women Organising*, London, Routledge.

Budig, M.J., 2014. *The Fatherhood Bonus and the Motherhood Penalty: Parenthood and the Gender Gap in Pay*, Washington, DC, Third Way.

Budig, M.J. and England, P., 2001. 'The Wage Penalty for Motherhood'. *American Sociological Review*, 66(2), pp. 204–225.

Bureau of Labor Statistics, U.S. Department of Labor, 2016, Paid Family Leave. Available at: www.bls.gov/opub/ted/2016/13-percent-of-private-industry-workers-had-access-to-paid-family-leave-in-march-2016.htm. Accessed: October 3 2018.

Calás, M.B. and Smircich, L., 1993. 'Dangerous Liaisons: The "Feminine-In-Management" Meets "Globalization"'. *Business Horizons*, 36(2), pp. 71–81.

Cameron, J. and Gibson-Graham, J.K., 2003. 'Feminising the Economy: Metaphors, Strategies, Politics'. *Gender, Place and Culture*, 10(2), pp. 145–157.

Cameron, K.S. and Quinn, R.E., 1999. *Diagnosing and Changing Organizational Culture*, Boston, MA, Addison-Wesley.

Castilla, E.J. and Benard, S., 2010. 'The Paradox of Meritocracy in Organizations'. *Administrative Science Quarterly*, 55(4), pp. 543–676.

Cech, E.A., 2013. 'Ideological Wage Inequalities? The Technical/Social Dualism and the Gender Wage Gap in Engineering'. *Social Forces*, 91(4), pp. 1147–1182.

Cech, E.A., 2015. 'Mechanism or Myth? Family Plans and the Reproduction of Occupational Gender Segregation'. *Gender and Society*, 30(2), pp. 265–288.

Chamberlain, L.J., Crowley, M., Tope, D., and Hodson, R., 2008. 'Sexual Harassment in Organizational Context'. *Work and Occupations*, 35(3), pp. 262–295.

Clarke, H.M. and Arnold, K.A., 2018. 'The Influence of Sexual Orientation on the Perceived Fit of Male Applicants for Both Male- and Female-Typed Jobs'. *Frontiers in Psychology*, 9, p. 656.

Cohen, P.N., 2013. 'The Persistence of Workplace Gender Segregation in the US'. *Sociology Compass*, 7(11), pp. 889–899.

Collins, P.H., 2017. 'On Violence, Intersectionality and Transversal Politics'. *Ethnic and Racial Studies*, 40(9), pp. 1460–1473.

Correll, S.J., 2001. 'Gender and the Career Choice Process: The Role of Biased Self-Assessments'. *American Journal of Sociology*, 106(6), pp. 1691–1730.

Correll, S.J., Benard, S., and Paik, I., 2007. 'Getting a Job: Is There a Motherhood Penalty?'. *American Journal of Sociology*, 112(5), pp. 1297–1339.

Cortina, L.M., Kabat-Farr, D., Leskinen, E.A., Huerta, M., and Magley, V.J., 2013. 'Selective Incivility as Modern Discrimination in Organizations: Evidence and Impact'. *Journal of Management*, 39(6), pp. 1579–1605.

Cox, T., 1993. *Cultural Diversity in Organizations: Theory, Research & Practice*, San Francisco, CA, Berrett-Koehler.

Deal, T. and Kennedy, A., 1984. *Corporate Cultures: The Rites and Rituals of Corporate Life*, New York, Basic Books.

Doering, L. and Thébaud, S., 2017. 'The Effects of Gendered Occupational Roles on Men's and Women's Workplace Authority: Evidence from Microfinance'. *American Sociological Review*, 82(3), pp. 542–567.

Dougherty, D.S. and Drumheller, K., 2006. 'Sensemaking and Emotions in Organizations: Accounting for Emotions in a Rational(ized) Context'. *Communication Studies*, 57(2), pp. 215–238.

Downey, K., 2009. *The Woman Behind the New Deal: The Life of Frances Perkins*, New York, Random House.

Duffy, M., 2007. 'Doing the Dirty Work Gender, Race, and Reproductive Labor in Historical Perspective'. *Gender and Society*, 21(3), pp. 313–336.

Durr, M. and Harvey Wingfield, A.M.H., 2011. 'Keep Your 'N' in Check: African American Women and the Interactive Effects of Etiquette and Emotional Labor'. *Critical Sociology*, 37(5), pp. 557–571.

Dutton, J.E. and Heaphy, E.D., 2003. 'The Power of High-Quality Connections'. In: K. Cameron and J. Dutton, ed., *Positive Organizational Scholarship: Foundations of a New Discipline*, Oakland, CA, Berrett-Koehler, pp. 262–278.

Eagly, A.H. and Karau, S.J., 2002. 'Role Congruity Theory of Prejudice Toward Female Leaders'. *Psychological Review*, 109(3), pp. 573–598.

Eagly, A.H., Makhijani, M.G., and Klonsky, B.G., 1992. 'Gender and the Evaluation of Leaders: A Meta-Analysis'. *Psychological Bulletin*, 111(1), pp. 3–22.

Economic Policy Institute, 2018, The Productivity–Pay Gap. Available at: www.epi.org/productivity-pay-gap/. Accessed October 22 2018.

Elsesser, K.M. and Lever, J., 2011. 'Does Gender Bias Against Female Leaders Persists? Quantitative and Qualitative Data from a Large-Scale Survey'. *Human Relations*, 64(12), pp. 1555–1578.

Ely, R. and Padavic, I., 2007. 'A Feminist Analysis of Organizational Research on Sex Differences'. *Academy of Management Review*, 32(4), pp. 1121–1143.

Ely, R.J., Ibarra, H., and Kolb, D.M., 2011. 'Taking Gender into Account: Theory and Design for Women's Leadership Development Programs'. *Academy of Management Learning and Education*, 10(3), pp. 474–493.

Farley, L., 1978. *Sexual Shakedown: The Sexual Harassment of Women in the Working World*, New York, McGraw-Hill.

Faulkner, W., 2000. 'Dualisms, Hierarchies, and Gender in Engineering'. *Social Studies of Science*, 30(5), pp. 759–792.

Federici, S., 2012. *Revolution at Point Zero: Housework, Reproduction, and Feminist Struggle*, Oakland, CA, Common Notions.

Ferber, M. and Nelson, J.A., 1993. *Beyond Economic Man: Feminist Theory and Economics*, Chicago, IL, University of Chicago Press.

Ferguson, K.E., 1984. *The Feminist Case Against Bureaucracy*, Philadelphia, PA, Temple University Press.

Ferguson, S., 2008. 'Canadian Contributions to Social Reproduction Feminism, Race, and Embodied Labor'. *Race, Gender and Class*, 15(1–2), pp. 42–57.

Fletcher, J.K., 1998. 'Relational Practice: A Feminist Reconstruction of Work'. *Journal of Management Inquiry*, 7(2), pp.163–186.

Fletcher, J.K., 1999. *Disappearing Acts: Gender, Power, and Relational. Practice at Work*, Cambridge, MA, MIT Press.

Fletcher, J.K., 2003. 'The Paradox of Post Heroic Leadership: Gender Matters', Center for Gender in Organizations Working Paper no. 17, Boston, MA, Simmons College.

Folbre, N., 2006. 'Measuring Care: Gender, Empowerment, and the Care Economy'. *Journal of Human Development*, 7(2), pp. 183–199.

Follett, M.P., 1924. *Creative Experience*, New York, Longmans.

Fraser, N., 2016. 'Contradictions of Capital and Care'. *New Left Review*, 100. Available at: https://newleftreview.org/II/100/nancy-fraser-contradictions-of-capital-and-care. Accessed: 10 October 2018.

Freeman, J., 1972. 'The Tyranny of Structurelessness'. *The Second Wave*, 2(1), p. 20.

Fried, J. and Hansson, D.H., 2018. *It Doesn't Have to Be Crazy at Work*, New York, Harper Business.

Gascoigne, C., Parry, E., and Buchanan, D., 2015. 'Extreme Work, Gendered Work? How Extreme Jobs and the Discourse of 'Personal Choice' Perpetuate Gender Inequality'. *Organization*, 22(4), pp. 457–475.

Gatrell, C., Cooper, C.L., and Kossek, E.E., 2017. 'Maternal Bodies as Taboo at Work: New Perspectives on the Marginalizing of Senior-Level Women in Organizations'. *Academy of Management Perspectives*, 31(3), pp. 239–252.

Gilligan, C., 1982. *In a Different Voice: Psychological Theory and Women's Development*, Cambridge, MA, Harvard University Press.

Gittell, J.H., 2006. 'Relational Coordination: Coordinating Work through Relationships of Shared Goals, Shared Knowledge and Mutual Respect'. In: O. Kyriakidou and M. Ozbilgin, eds, *Relational Perspectives in Organizational Studies: A Research Companion*, London, Edward Elgar, pp. 336–357, Ch. 5.

Gittell, J.H. and Douglass, A., 2012. 'Relational Bureaucracy: Structuring Reciprocal Relationships into Roles'. *Academy of Management Review*, 37(4), pp. 709–733.

Glick, P. and Fiske, S.T., 2001. 'An Ambivalent Alliance. Hostile and Benevolent Sexism as Complementary Justifications for Gender Inequality'. *The American Psychologist*, 56(2), pp. 109–118.

Graham, P., 1995. *Mary Parker Follett: Prophet of Management*, Boston, MA, Harvard Business School Press.

Halley, J., Kotiswaran, P., Rebouché, R., and Shamir, H., 2018. *Governance Feminism: An Introduction*, Minneapolis, MN, University of Minnesota Press.

Harquail, C.V., 2017. Introducing the Feminist Business Model Canvas. Available at: www.cvharquail.com/feminist-business-tools-1/. Accessed: October 18 2018.

Hartmann, H., 1976. 'Capitalism, Patriarchy, and Job Segregation by Sex'. *Signs*, 1(3, Part 2), pp. 137–169

Hassard, J., Holliday, R., and Willmott, H., 2000. *Body and Organization*, London, Sage.

Hatch, M.J. and Schultz, M., 1996. 'Living with Multiple Paradigms: The Case of Paradigm Interplay in Organizational Culture Studies'. *Academy of Management Review*, 21(2), pp. 529–557.

Hearn, J., Sheppard, D., Tancred, P., and Burrell, G., 1989. *The Sexuality of Organization*, London, Sage.

Hegewisch, A., Phil, M., and Ellis, E., 2015. The Gender Wage Gap by Occupation 2014 and by Race and Ethnicity. Available at: https://iwpr.org/publications/the-gender-wage-gap-by-occupation-2014-and-by-race-and-ethnicity/. Accessed: October 2 2018.

Heilman, M.E. and Chen, J.J., 2005. 'Same Behavior, Different Consequences: Reactions to Men's and Women's Altruistic Citizenship Behavior'. *The Journal of Applied Psychology*, 90(3), pp. 431–441.

Heilman, M.E. and Okimoto, T.G., 2007. 'Why Are Women Penalized for Success at Male Tasks?: The Implied Communality Deficit'. *The Journal of Applied Psychology*, 92(1), pp. 81–92.

Heim, P., 1992. *Hardball for Women: Winning at the Game of Business*. Los Angeles, CA, Lowell House.

Helgesen, S., 1995. *The Web of Inclusion: A New Architecture for Building Great Organizations*, New York, Doubleday Business.

Hesmondhalgh, D. and Baker, S., 2015, 'Sex, Gender and Work Segregation in the Cultural Industries'. *The Sociological Review*, 63(Suppl 1), pp. 23–36.

Hirst, A. and Schwabenland, C., 2018. 'Doing Gender in the 'New Office'. *Gender, Work and Organization*, 25(2), pp. 159–176.

Hochschild, A., 1983. *The Managed Heart: Commercialization of Human Feeling*, Berkeley, CA, University of California Press.

Hochschild, A., 2000. 'Global Care Chains and Emotional Surplus Value'. In: W. Hutton and A. Giddens, eds, *On the Edge: Living with Global Capitalism*, London, Jonathan Cape, pp. 131–146.

Hulin, C.L., Fitzgerald, L.F., and Drasgow, F., 1996. 'Organizational Influences on Sexual Harassment'. In: M.S. Stockdale, ed., *Women and Work: A Research and Policy Series, Vol. 5. Sexual Harassment in the Workplace: Perspectives, Frontiers, and Response Strategies*, Thousand Oaks CA, Sage Publications, Inc., pp. 127–150, Ch. 7.

Hult, K.M., 1995. 'Feminist Organization Theories and Government Organizations: The Promise of Diverse Structural Forms'. *Public Productivity and Management Review*, 19(2), pp. 128–142.

Iannello, K.P., 1992. *Decisions Without Hierarchy: Feminist Interventions in Organization Theory and Practice*, New York, Routledge.

Institute for Women's Policy Research (IWPR), 2015. The Gender Wage Gap by Occupation 2014 and by Race and Ethnicity. Available at: https://iwpr.org/publications/the-gender-wage-gap-by-occupation-2014-and-by-race-and-ethnicity/. Accessed: October 10 2018.

Institute for Women's Policy Research (IWPR), 2016. The Economic Impact of Equal Pay by State. Available at: https://iwpr.org/publications/the-economic-impact-of-equal-pay-by-state/. Accessed: October 10 2018.

Jean-Marie, G., Williams, V.A., and Sherman, S.L., 2009. 'Black Women's Leadership Experiences: Examining the Intersectionality of Race and Gender'. *Advances in Developing Human Resources*, 11(5), pp. 562–581.

Just Associates, 2016. How Does Feminist Change Happen? Training Tools and How-to. Available at: https://justassociates.org/en/resources/training-tools-how-tos. Accessed: October 18 2018.

Kanter, R.M., 1977. *Men and Women of the Corporation*, New York, Basic Books.

Kelliher, C. and Anderson, D., 2010. 'Doing More with Less? Flexible Working Practices and the Intensification of Work'. *Human Relations*, 63(1), pp. 83–106.

Kelly, M., 2003. *The Divine Right of Capital: Dethroning the Corporate Elite*, Oakland, CA, Berrett-Koehler.

King, E.B., Botsford, W., Hebl, M.R., Kazama, S., Dawson, J.F., and Perkins, A., 2012. 'Benevolent Sexism at Work: Gender Differences in the Distribution of Challenging Developmental Experiences'. *Journal of Management*, 38(6), pp. 1835–1866.

Klenke, K., 2011. *Women in Leadership: Contextual Dynamics and Boundaries*, Bingley, UK, Emerald Group Publishing.

Koen, S., 1984. *Feminist Workplaces: Alternative Models for the Organization of Work*, Unpublished PhD dissertation, Union for Experimental Colleges, Union Graduate School, The Union for Experimenting Colleges and Universities, Cincinnati, OH.

Kossek, E.E., Su, R., and Wu, L., 2017. '"Opting Out" or "Pushed Out?" Integrating Perspectives on Women's Career Equality for Gender Inclusion and Interventions'. *Journal of Management*, 41(1), pp. 228–254.

Kreeger, L. and Holloway, E., 2008. 'Now You See It and Now You Don't: Consequences of Veiling Relational Work'. *Ethnographic Praxis in Industry Conference Proceedings*, 2008(1), pp. 31–39.

Kricheli-Katz, T., 2012. 'Choice, Discrimination, and the Motherhood Penalty'. *Law and Society Review*, 46(3), pp. 557–587.

Kunda, G., 2006. *Engineering Culture: Control and Commitment in a High-Tech Corporation*, Philadelphia, PA, Temple University Press.

Laslett, B. and Brenner, J., 1989. 'Gender and Social Reproduction: Historical Perspectives'. *Annual Review of Sociology*, 15, pp. 381–404.

Lee, R., 2018. 'Breastfeeding Bodies: Intimacies at Work'. *Gender, Work and Organization*, 25(1), pp. 77–90.

Levanon, A., England, P., and Allison, P., 2009. 'Occupational Feminization and Pay: Assessing Causal Dynamics Using 1950–2000 US Census Data'. *Social Forces*, 88(2), pp. 865–891.

Liedtka, J.M., 1996. 'Feminist Morality and Competitive Reality: A Role for an Ethic of Care?'. *Business Ethics Quarterly*, 6(2), pp. 179–200.

Lipman-Blumen, J., 1992. 'Connective Leadership: Female Leadership Styles in the 21st-Century Workplace'. *Sociological Perspectives*, 35(1), pp. 183–203.

Lynch, K., Baker, K., and Lyons, M., 2009. *Affective Equality: Love, Care and Injustice*, New York, Palgrave Macmillan.

Machold, S., Ahmed, P.K., and Farquhar, S.S., 2008. 'Corporate Governance and Ethics: A Feminist Perspective'. *Journal of Business Ethics*, 81(3), pp. 665–678.

MacKinnon, C.A., 1978. *Sexual Harassment of Working Women: A Case of Sex Discrimination*, New Haven, CT, Yale University Press.

Maddock, S. and Parkin, D., 1993. 'Gender Cultures: Women's Choices and Strategies at Work'. *Women in Management Review*, 8(2), pp. 3–9.

Martin, J., 1992. *Cultures in Organizations: Three Perspectives*, Oxford, UK, Oxford University Press.

Martin, J., Knopoff, K., and Beckman, C., 1998. 'An Alternative to Bureaucratic Impersonality and Emotional Labor: Bounded Emotionality at the Body Shop'. *Administrative Science Quarterly*, 43(2), pp. 429–469.

Mavin, S. and Grandy, G., 2016. 'Women Elite Leaders Doing Respectable Business Femininity: How Privilege is Conferred, Contested and Defended through the Body'. *Gender, Work and Organization*, 23(4), pp. 379–396.

McKinney, C., 2015. 'Newsletter Networks in the Feminist History and Archives Movement'. *Feminist Theory*, 16(3), pp. 309–328.

Memon, N.Z. and Jena, L.K., 2017. 'Gender Inequality, Job Satisfaction and Job Motivation: Evidence from Indian Female Employees'. *Management and Labour Studies*, 42(3), pp. 253–274.

Mumby, D.K. and Putnam, L.L., 1992. 'The Politics of Emotion: A Feminist Reading of Bounded Rationality'. *Academy of Management Review*, 17(3), pp. 465–486.

Nadal, K.L., 2008. 'Preventing Racial, Ethnic, Gender, Sexual Minority, Disability, and Religious Microaggressions'. *Prevention in Counseling Psychology: Theory, Research, Practice and Training*, 2(1), pp. 22–27.

National Women's Law Center (NWLC), 2016. The Wage Gap: The Who, How, Why, and What to Do. Available at: https://nwlc.org/resources/the-wage-gap-the-who-how-why-and-what-to-do/. Accessed: October 18 2018.

Nohria, N., 1995. Mary Parker Follett's View on Power, the Giving of Orders, and Authority: An Altenrative to Hierarchy or a Utopian Ideology? In P. Graham, ed., *Mary Parker Follett, Prophet of Management: A Celebration of Writings from the 1920s*, Washington, DC: Beard Books, pp. 154–162.

Notter, J. and Grant, M., 2011. *Humanize: How People-Centric Organizations Succeed in a Social World*, Indianapolis, IN, Que Publishing.

O'Mahony, S., 2018. 'Understanding Mary Parker Follett (1868–1933)'. In: *Classics of Management Theory PDW: Highlighting the Relevance of Earlier Scholarship for*

Contemporary Research, Paper presented at the Academy of Management Annual Meeting, August, Chicago, IL.

Padavic, I., Ely, R.J., and Reid, E.M., 2019. 'Explaining the Persistence of Gender Inequality: The Work-Family Narrative as a Social Defense against the 24/7 Work Culture'. *Administrative Science Quarterly*, in press.

Paludi, M., Helms Mills, J., and Mills, A.J., 2014. 'Disturbing Thoughts and Gendered Practices: A Discursive Review of Feminist Organizational Analysis'. In: S. Kumra, R. Simpson, and R.J. Burke, eds, *The Oxford Handbook of Gender and Organizations*, Oxford, UK, Oxford University Press, pp. 53–75.

Parker, P.J., 2006. *Race, Gender, and Leadership: Re-envisioning Organizational Leadership from the Perspectives of African American Women Executives*, Mahwah, NJ, Lawrence Erlbaum.

Pierce, C., Carew, J., Pierce-Gonzalez, D., and Willis, D., 1978. 'An Experiment in Racism: TV Commercials'. In: C. Pierce, ed., *Television and Education*, Beverly Hills, CA, Sage, pp. 62–88.

Pietrykowski, B., 2017. 'Revaluing Low-Wage Work: Service-Sector Skills and the Fight for 15'. *Review of Radical Political Economics*, 49(1), pp. 5–29.

Plaskow, J., 2008. 'Embodiment, Elimination and the Role of Toilets in Struggles for Social Justice'. *Crosscurrents*, 58(1), pp. 51–64.

Power, M., 2004. 'Social Provisioning as a Starting Point for Feminist Economics'. *Feminist Economics*, 10(3), pp. 3–19.

Prieto, L.C., Phipps, S.T.A., Thompson, L.R., and Smith, X.A., 2016. 'Schneiderman, Perkins, and the Early Labor Movement: An Ethic of Care Approach to Labor and Safety Reform'. *Journal of Management History*, 22(1), pp. 50–72.

Pringle, R., 1993. 'Male Secretaries'. In: C.L. Williams, ed., *Doing "Women's Work": Men in Nontraditional Occupations*, Thousand Oaks, CA, Sage, pp. 128–151, Ch. 8.

Pullen, A. and Rhodes, C., 2015. 'Ethics, Embodiment and Organizations'. *Organization*, 22(2), pp. 159–165.

Rafaeli, A., Dutton, J., Harquail, C., and Mackie-Lewis, S., 1997. 'Navigating by Attire: The Use of Dress by Female Administrative Employees'. *Academy of Management Journal*, 40(1), pp. 9–47.

Reskin, B.F., 1988. 'Bringing the Men Back in: Sex Differentiation and the Devaluation of Women's Work'. *Gender and Society*, 2(1), pp. 58–81.

Ridgeway, C.L., 2011. *Framed by Gender: How Gender Inequality Persists in the Modern World*, New York, Oxford University Press.

Riger, S., 1994. 'Challenges of Success: Stages of Growth in Feminist Organizations'. *Feminist Studies*, 20(2), pp. 275–300.

Roddick, A., 1991. *Body and Soul: Profits with Principles*, New York, Crown.

Rosener, J.B., 1990. 'Ways Women Lead'. *Harvard Business Review*, 68(6), pp. 119–125.

Rudman, L.A., 1998. 'Self-Promotion as a Risk Factor for Women: The Costs and Benefits of Counterstereotypical Impression Management'. *Journal of Personality and Social Psychology*, 74(3), pp. 629–645.

Salin, D., 2003. 'The Significance of Gender in the Prevalence, Forms and Perceptions of Workplace Bullying'. *Nordiske Organisasjonsstudier*, 5(3), pp. 30–50.

Schein, E., 2010. *Organizational Culture and Leadership*, San Francisco, CA, Jossey-Bass.

Schultz, V., 1998. 'Sex Is the Least of It – Let's Focus Harassment Law on Work, Not Sex'. *The Nation*, 266(19), pp. 11–15.

Schultz, V. and Hoffman, A., 2006. 'The Need for a Reduced Workweek in the United States'. In: J. Fudge and R. Owens, eds., *Precarious Work, Women, and the New Economy*, New York, Bloomsbury Publishing.

Selmi, P. and Hunter, R., 2001. 'Beyond the Rank and File Movement: Mary van Kleeck and Social Work Radicalism in the Great Depression'. *The Journal of Sociology and Social Welfare*, 28(2), Article 6, pp. 11–15.

Seron, C., Silbey, S., Cech, E., and Rubineau, B., 2018. 'I am Not a Feminist, but... : Hegemony of a Meritocratic Ideology and the Limits of Critique Among Women in Engineering'. *Work and Occupations*, 45(2), pp. 131–167.

Sherman, K.E., 2015. Black Americans' Experiences of Incivility in the Workplace: An Extension and Reconceptualization of the Workplace Incivility Scale. Available at: https://scholarworks.umass.edu/dissertations_2/40. Accessed: October 12 2018.

Shirley, S., 2012. *Let IT Go: The Memoirs of Dame Stephanie Shirley*, London, Acorn Books.

Sinclair, A., 2014. 'A Feminist Case for Leadership'. In: J. Damousi, K. Rubenstein and M. Tomsic, eds, *Diversity in Leadership: Australian Women Past and Present*, Canberra, Australia, Australian National University ePress, pp. 17–35. DOI:10.22459/DL.11.2014.01. Accessed: October 20 2018.

Sojo, V.E., Wood, R.E., and Genat, A.E., 2016. 'Harmful Workplace Experiences and Women's Occupational Well-Being: A Meta-Analysis'. *Psychology of Women Quarterly*, 40(1), pp. 10–40.

Superville, D.R., 2016. Few Women Run the Nation's School Districts. Why? Available at: www.edweek.org/ew/articles/2016/11/16/few-women-run-the-nations-school-districts.html. Accessed: October 20 2018.

Tilcsik, A., Anteby, M., and Knight, C.R., 2015. 'Concealable Stigma and Occupational Segregation: Toward a Theory of Gay and Lesbian Occupations'. *Administrative Science Quarterly*, 60(3), pp. 446–481.

Tronto, J., 2017. 'There Is an Alternative: *Homines Curans* and the Limits of Neoliberalism'. *International Journal of Care and Caring*, 1(1), pp. 27–43.

Tronto, J.C. and Fisher, B., 1990. 'Toward a Feminist Theory of Caring'. In: E. Abel and M. Nelson, eds, *Circles of Care*, Albany, NY, SUNY Press, pp. 36–54.

U.S. Department of Labor, 2016. Working Mothers Issue Brief. Available at: www.dol.gov/wb/resources/WB_WorkingMothers_508_FinalJune13.pdf. Accessed: October 20 2018.

U.S. Department of Labor, 2017. Occupational Employment and Wages, May 2017. Available at: www.bls.gov/oes/current/oes372012.htm. Accessed: October 20 2018.

U.S. Equal Employment Opportunity Commission, 2016. Select Task Force on the Study of Harassment in the Workplace. Available at: www.eeoc.gov/eeoc/task_force/harassment/upload/report.pdf. Accessed: October 20 2018.

University of California Berkeley (UCB) Labor Center, 2015. The High Public Cost of Low Wages. Available at: http://laborcenter.berkeley.edu/the-high-public-cost-of-low-wages/. Accessed: October 20 2018.

Vogel, L., 2014. *Marxism and the Oppression of Women: Towards a Unitary Theory*, Chicago, IL, Haymarket.

Wharton, A.S., 2009. 'The Sociology of Emotional Labor'. *Annual Review of Sociology*, 35(1), pp. 147–165.

Wheeler, C.E. and Chinn, P.L., 1991. *Peace and Power: A Handbook of Feminist Process*, Washington, DC, National League for Nursing.

Williams, C.L., Giuffre, P.A., and Dellinger, K., 1999. 'Sexuality in the Workplace: Organizational Control, Sexual Harassment, and the Pursuit of Pleasure'. *Annual Review of Sociology*, 25(1), pp. 73–93.

Williams, J.C., 1991. 'Dissolving the Sameness/Difference Debate: A Post-Modern Path beyond Essentialism in Feminist and Critical Race Theory'. *Duke Law Journal*, 1991(2), pp. 296–323.

Williams, J.C., 2004. 'Hitting the Maternal Wall'. *Academe*, 90(6), pp. 16–20.

Williams, K.S. and Mills, A.J., 2017. 'Frances Perkins: Gender, Context and History in the Neglect of a Management Theorist'. *Journal of Management History*, 23(1), pp. 32–50.

Wolkowitz, C., 2006. *Bodies at Work*, London, Sage.

Worline, M.C. and Dutton, J.E., 2017. *Awakening Compassion at Work: The Quiet Power That Elevates People and Organizations*, Oakland, CA, Berrett-Koehler.

CONCLUSION

This book has encouraged you to look at the world of business and management a little differently, with a consideration of some important challenges, to invite you to consider what kind of positive force business could become.

The primer on feminism should have dispelled any reservations you might have had about whether feminism is a good thing. The definition of feminism as ending sexism, establishing equality, and creating flourishing, along with the feminist values of agency, equality, whole humanness, generativity, and interindependence, is completely positive. Feminism's goals are not scary – who could be afraid of flourishing? And they aren't exclusive – women, men, and all people benefit from feminist advocacy. The only potential losers are those with privilege they haven't earned, and their losses will be temporary while they learn to adjust to the greater, shared benefits of collective flourishing.

You now have some key concepts, some useful language, and some business-oriented example analyses that you can apply on your own to topics we haven't had room to address here. You should feel equipped to handle questions from other business people about feminism, and to reanalyze what you've been taught both about feminism and especially about business. Outfitted with a better understanding of feminism, you should also be able to anticipate the positive ways that feminism can influence and help to transform business.

To pursue a future of flourishing, we don't have to give up on working together, making things together, inventing innovative products, selling things to earn a profit, and using those profits to support ourselves, our families and our communities. We don't have to give up on challenging ourselves, on demonstrating personal initiative, or on pursuing individual achievement and success.

However, it's time to think about life beyond profit and beyond efficiency. It's also time to develop concerns larger than marketplace disruption or domination and consider what it would mean for all of us to have businesses that help us flourish.

It's time to start being creative and audacious about what business could be. It's time to invite business to be a force for positive social and economic change. Let's define these business and personal goals in ways that harm none of us and benefit all of us.

It may be difficult to envision what the world would look like with profitable businesses run by employees who participate, coordinate, and benefit as peers, rather than imagining businesses as towers of ladders winnowing out the weak in a race to the top, all to generate wealth for a tiny few. The difficulty of envisioning a radically different model isn't a failure of your imagination, but rather shows the power of the neoliberal, postfeminist, and late-stage capitalist world views that make alternatives seem implausible or impossible.

We are up against some pretty entrenched ideas, ideas that have taught us to treat them as inevitable. But they are no more inevitable than a man being disqualified from leadership positions because he's balding.

From both the overview of organizational approaches to gender equality and the essays on core management concepts, it is clear business is stuck in negative patterns of its own creation. The internal problems that companies are trying to solve are created by illegitimate power imbalances, unearned privilege, and gendered bias. These not only impede progress towards gender equality, but also prevent business from exploring the opportunities that might come from a focus on flourishing. No amount of repair will eliminate the symptoms; the only lasting cure is wholesale, transformational change.

Perhaps the biggest falsehood we are peddled by the anti-feminist, anti-flourishing stewards of the status quo is that equality and justice are at odds with profitable business. Maybe it is true that conventional business can't grow profits and returns on investment for everyone without relying on extractive practices or working against the interests of the majority. Maybe it is true that conventional business depends on dominance and oppression just like drains depend on gravity. But if this is the case, there's no reason to accept it and keep hoping that if we work hard enough, we'll beat the odds and make our way into the privileged elite, to become one of the few folks for whom the system seems to work. We have other options that are far more promising.

Feminism offers practices and visions that will help to heal the problems businesses face internally, as well as the problems business causes in our lives, our communities, and our ecosystems. We don't have to know now exactly what the steps are, we just need to know in general and in principle what we seek, and start there. We seek to end sexism and oppression, to establish equality and agency, and to create a world where everyone flourishes. Feminism offers one strong light to illuminate a path, and other anti-oppression movements offer other lights, all pointing towards the same goal. You can work with feminism, or you can work with another anti-oppression perspective, as long as you move forward.

Three action options to consider:

First, you can examine the bropropriated and colonized "progressive" business initiatives you've already seen advertised, and consider how to return these to their political, transformative roots. Look at newly "discovered" feminist ideas in management and ask what the colonizers missed or what they misconstrued. Raise the question, for example, if it makes sense to ask employees to be positive and engaged without addressing the jobs that continue to extract as much as they can from each of us. Ask whether any organizational initiatives address types of oppression beyond just gender, and if they don't, ask how they can.

Second, you can look in your own work, job, team, department, and company for ways to demonstrate feminist values and step forward towards gender equality and flourishing. Maybe you can respect whole humanness by helping your team set goals that don't depend on late nights at the office or punishing travel schedules, or support generativity by looking for ways that each member can contribute something meaningful to a project while distributing the boring work of the project more fairly. You could continue to learn about feminism and about feminist work practices (see FeministsAtWork. com for ideas). Every person can play a role in establishing gender equality and moving towards flourishing in their workplace.

Third, you can follow the lead of entrepreneurial feminists who are already building profitable businesses that put feminist values and the goal of flourishing into practice. These companies are using feminist principles to design their technology, to build their products, to test their ideas with customers, and to craft positive, ennobling marketing messages that draw customers to them. These companies are granting ownership pegged to employee tenure, holding community-wide conversations about serious company issues, and sharing decision making broadly. These companies are earning enough revenue to pay everyone fairly and return some – but not most – profit to their investors (see some examples on my website cvharquail.com, along with reading lists and learning resources). Examples are out there. Let them inspire you.

We are inside a circle whose magic – if you want to call it magic and not sleight of hand – prevents us from even thinking about the right questions to ask. But feminism is asking these questions. Feminist interventions don't claim to have all the answers, but they do raise the quality of the questions we all should be asking. Feminism challenges how we think about who people are, what they care about, what they have to offer, how best to invite them to contribute, and how best to lead with them in the shared work of creating value. Feminism also challenges how we think about value itself, what contributes to value, how contributions to value should be compensated, and how humans' efforts (energy, meaning, time, life) to create value should be balanced against the importance of money and power. *Feminism is not only asking these questions. Feminism is also inviting you to answer them, in concert with your coworkers, community members, and the stakeholders to whom you are responsible.*

Feminism has ideas for transforming the magic circle, to embrace the interests of every living creature and promote a vision of flourishing for the whole. Feminism is out to change the rules of the game. You should be, too.

INDEX

Page numbers in **bold** refer to tables.